D1881005

Land Development and Good Governance

Land Development and Good Governance:

Practice and Challenges

Dr. Karanam Viswa Bhushan

GenNext Publication

© **Author**

All rights reserved. No part of this work may be reproduced, stored, adapted, or transmitted in any form or by any means, electronic, mechanical, photocopying, micro-filming, recording or otherwise, or translated in any language, without the prior written permission of the copyright owner and the publisher. The book is sold subject to the condition that it shall not, by way of trade or otherwise, be lent, resold, hired out, or otherwise circulated without the prior publisher's written consent in any form of binding or cover other than that in which it is published.

The views and opinions expressed in this book are author(s) own and the facts reported by them have been verified to the extent possible, and the publishers are not in any way liable for the same.

First Published, 2021

Published by

GenNext Publication
5, Ansari Road
Daryaganj, New Delhi-110002
Phone: 9811692060
E-mail: gennextpublication@hotmail.com

Printed at: Gyan Press, Delhi.

Cataloging in Publication Data—DK
Courtesy: D.K. Agencies (P) Ltd. <docinfo@dkagencies.com>

Bhushan, Karanam Viswa, 1963- **author.**
Land development and good governance : practice and challenges / Dr. Karanam Viswa Bhushan.
pages cm
Includes bibliographical references.
ISBN 9789353243265 (HB)
"An Imprint of Kalpaz Publication"

1. Real estate development—Ethiopia. 2. Ethiopia—Politics and government. 3. Economic development—Ethiopia. I. Title.

LCC HD1390.B48 2021 | DDC 333.73150963 23

Contents

Acknowledgements

I would thank the Almighty God for all his blessings and heavenly support

I would like to express my gratitude to all the people who have helped to complete the task of book publication.

I would like to thank my student Ethiopa Negash for her involvement and participation in the research work

It is pleasure to express my thanks to the staff of concerned office for providing the necessary information.

I would like to express my deep sense of gratitude to my elder brother K.V.A. Prasad Rao and his family for his inspiration and encouragement.

List of Tables

List of Figures

Chapter One

Introduction

Good governance is held to be the foundation of growth with in several democratic form of regime. Good governance is one of the greatest element in every nation. This chapter deals with the general background, statement of the problem, objectives, and significance of the study. It also consists of the scope and limitation of the study.

1.1. Background of the Study

Good Governance could be a key part in development and in guaranteeing that economic process of all benefits in society. The state, in partnership with civil society and personal sector, encompasses a major role to play within the look for peace, bigger freedom, social equity and property development. Additionally it includes awareness at operational level, inclusiveness, transparency and answerability. These components area unit reciprocally reinforcing and can't stand alone. Good governance additionally promotes the rule of law (Shrestha, 2000).

Here, governance is delineated the method of decision and therefore the process by that selections area unit enforced or not enforced and it will apply to company, international, national, native governance or to the interactions between different sectors of society.

These days, it's typically accepted that, good governance is a necessary precondition for Sustainable development. Different countries in that area quite similar in terms of their natural resources and structure have shown totally different performance in raising the welfare of their individuals. Much of this can be owing to standards of governance. Poor governance stifles and impedes development, wherever there's corruption, poor management of public funds, lack of answerableness, abuses of human rights and excessive military influence.

Downer (2000) cited in Mulusew (2013), it is important to differentiate good governance from different ideas that seem parallel, like growth and economic process. Its place of considering them as equal, several scholars argue them as options that area unit probable to be connected in numerous ways. In fact, the importance that authors provide to sensible governance is because of the impact it is going to wear development and economic enlargement.

According to Grindle (2004), the significance of receiving good governance comes precisely from its relationship with the event of a rustic and therefore the reduction of economic condition. Not only Setting associate degree agenda to realize good governance. However complex task, that makes the author to propose rather a "good governance" agenda as a start line. within the building of this simple agenda, the thought is to come back policies that have worked within the past, set priorities during a deliberately approach, believe policies with larger impact in assuaging economic condition and achieving development, and appearance for innovative ways in which of implement such policy.

In terms of economic process, there good measure many authors linking that variable with good governance, however within the sense of "being connected to" rather than "being half of". In alternative words, scholars are intrigue by the connection between good governance and economic or political development. As Grindle (2007) mentioned there are many measures to be found among indicators of good governance and economic process, On the other hand those associations difficult to determine even tougher to be attributed as causative. However, she mentions the work of Kauffman (2002) who found a causative and positive association between completely different scope of good governance and therefore the GDP per capita within the long haul, i.e. good governance makes development sustainable.

These scope good governance however the government is elective and overseeing, the responsibility power of voters, the believability within the government, the respect for establishments, each from management and voters, and therefore the effective delivery of public merchandise. He found that the relative between these two variables doesn't hold within the reverse direction, It implies that higher levels of economic process don't result in higher governance. For instance, Quain (2003) points out that China and Vietnam are frequent samples of countries that have created outstanding leaps in economic development and financial condition reduction.

Good governance in the context of many country the wide expression to locate exclusive definition. According to Fukuyama (2013) there are two dimensions to qualify governance as good or bad: the capability of the state and the bureaucracy's autonomy, both of them complement, when the state is more capable, for instance through the compilation of taxes, there should be more autonomy, because the bureaucrats are able to conduct things well without being instructed with a lot of details. In less capable states, however, less discretion and more rules setting are attractive. Another way of thinking about good governance is through outcomes.

Since Governments carry out with goals like the provision of public goods to its citizens, there is no better way to think about good governance other than through deliverables, which are precisely the one demanded by citizens, like security, health, education, water, the enforcement of contracts, protection to property, protection to the environment and their capability to vote and get paid fair wages.

In Ethiopia Good Governance is a challenge in various regimes. For instance, in Haile Selassie regime, Ethiopia has been highly national monarchical management. The central government created coordination with the limited elite with the only objectives of centralize the government and as result citizens remained without empowerment. In Dergi regime the middle government system sustained and there was lack of responsibility to the nation and the public service lack independence (USAID 2013) cited as (Zelalem, 2016).

Before 1991, the theme of good governance is not given due stress by the governments of the country. Ethiopia, after a long year's custom of federal government and governance structure, a decentralization form of government and governance arrangement has been adopt in 1991 with four government agreement, Federal, Regional, Woreda and Kebele.

Generally, the researcher understand that good governance, in Ethiopians has be obtain attention after coming power in May 1991 through various measures to reform the public sector. This shows the government commitment towards the implementation of good governance to bring fair responsible, effective, efficient, ethical and civil service that promotes good governance. However, the government committed to use different phases of tools or methods to achieve strategic goals there are so many gaps up to date. As stated in different theoretical reviews' there are less leadership commitment and support to achieve good governance to give quality service delivery and as shown practical performance measurement report in study area Bole sub city administration the study with municipality of Addis Ababa and sub cities in 2016/2017 in lower stage as sub city level and in each sectors and CSA 2015/2016 survey displays lower by citizen satisfaction. Therefore, the study with practice and challenges of good governance in Bole Sub City administration. Finally, the researcher proposed recommendations that can contribute for sub city to success of Good /Governance.

1.2. Statement of the Problem

Currently different document have stress the suggestion of good governance in public sector. The main beliefs of good governance practice are expected open and progressive policy building, accountable and clear process of qualified culture that combat corruption, bias, nepotism and individual gain and strict economic control and administration of funding. It is clear that correctly set up and execution of good governance principles may also many of the problems come across in public sector.

According Seidman. (2007) cited by Zelalem (2016) Good Governance has major role in attractive the economic, social and political development., Insure good governance is a extremely challenging duty by different reason. It has exaggerated through lack of institutional capability, competent individual authority, financial capacity and current technology resulted in poor service delivery.

According to Melese (2013) in Ethiopia, the challenges of good governance in practice are the accountability of employees to their responsibilities that is not guided by rules, lack of public participation in government activities, lack of impartial treatment, lack of leadership who are modeling the way to enhance good governance>>.

Applying good governance results enhanced service delivery, attract investment, minimize corruption, and promote community involvement in decision making and accountability and also increases common sense of ownership within citizens. It leads to additional fair allocation of property and promote more sustainable and well-organized consumption of resources there by raise sense of equality and safety of citizens (World Bank 1992)

As the researcher observation shows that the level of attentiveness about leadership of how and when the society involving on good governance is low. Among, public officers are not accountable for the decision making they complete, slight involvement of society in decision making procedure with the intention of community are decision taker rather than decision maker, the fulfillment level of customer is too little also there is dissatisfaction of stockholders in the organization and rampant corruption will occur (Bole sub city Land Development and Management office report, (2016, 2017) and the researcher also has experience in working on the sub-city as expert and head of different Sector. The researcher observed a serious problem on practices and challenges of good governance in land development and management office from the perspective of transparency, accountability, participation,. efficiency and effectiveness To do so the presences of committed as well as visionary leadership and civil servant who can articulate values and believes of customer satisfaction becomes on extremely critical requirement or precondition to achieve objective of good governance. The researcher finds out solution to recommended Bole Sub city administration on topic of practice and challenges of good governance.

1.3. Research Questions

The study will guide by the following research questions;

1. What are the current practices of good governance in terms of transparency, accountability, participation, efficiency and effectiveness in Bole Sub City Land Development and Management office?
2. What are the challenges hindering implementation of good governance principles in case of service delivery in Bole Sub City Land Development and Management office?
3. What is the solution for existing challenges?

1.4. Objectives of the Study

1.4.1. General Objective of the Study

The general objective of the study is to assess the Practices and Challenges implementing of Good governance principles in Addis Ababa specifically in Bole Sub City Land Development and Management Office.

1.4.2. Specific Objectives of the Study

This study specifically, attempts to:

1. Describe the current practices of good governance principles from the perspective of transparency accountability, participation, efficiency and effectiveness in Bole Sub City Land Development and Management office
2. Assess the major challenges for implementation of good governance in the office
3. Propose the solution for the challenges

1.5. Significant of the Study

The central of this study is to assess practices and challenges of good governance in the public organizations by taking a case of Bole sub-city Land Development and Management

Office. Thus, the findings of this study will be useful to the stakeholders including:

- **Leaders**: the research findings will help the leaders of the sub-city to overcome challenges faced in implementing good governance in the sub-city.
- **Customers:** Customers of the organization are beneficiary from the study through identified problem and set solution.
- **Future researcher***:* The study also uses as a reference for those who are interested to conduct further study on the problem. It will also be an indicative document and may develop empirical data.

1.6. Scope of the Study

Even though, City Government of Addis Ababa has ten Sub-Cities and one hundred seventeen Woredas administration employ thousands of employees to provide that civil service to public, this study is delimited only to one sub-city administration. A time and resource limitation makes it practically difficult to consider other Sub Cities for the study. On the other hand, the study focused on Bole sub-city administration because of the researcher familiarity with this locality. It will be convenient to distribute and collect questionnaire and obtain relevant documents in a timely manner. Furthermore, the study is mainly focusing on five principles of good governance. Namely, Transparency, Accountability, Participation, efficiency and effectiveness. Implementation of these are a precondition and important. The remaining principles will follow as well. The researcher believes that the selected good governance pillars will help to indirectly make sure observance for the remaining principles. The respondents in this study will be limited to only Bole sub city Land Development and Management office employee, service users and managers, the findings may not be generalized to other sub cities with certainty.

1.7. Limitation of the Study

The main limitation during the survey conducted would be lack of necessary document from the organization to use as a reference, Lack of adequate information regarding to the role of leaders to ensure good governance, un addressed issues, Some respondents will be unwilling to fill the questionnaire and return back,. On the other hand leaders have not obtained enough time for interview. To overcome the limitation, the researcher will apply different methods such as applying self-administer data collection method to collect data rapidly from respondents within a short period of time and meeting the respondents particularly the leaders out of the operating times together with weekends and also the investigator can make a case for totally the target in regard to the event of the country.

1.8. Definition of Terms

This section provides definitions for terms in the thesis that are unusual and those terms will be using in a specific way per the objective of the study:

Governance refers to applying of political and managerial power at each and every one levels to mange a country's associations. (UNDP 2012)

Good Governance: to implement ability through political and institutional procedure that is clear and accountable and support public contribution (UJN 2007),

Land Tenure: the term tenure is derived from a Latin term for holding or possessing land. Therefore land tenure reflects to the manner in which land rights are held, used and transacted (Bruce, 1998)

Land Management: the exploit linked through the supervision of land as resources from together an ecological and financial point of view, towards sustainable development (UN, 1999)

Land Administration: means the process of determining, recording, and disseminating information about tenure, value, and use of land when implementing land management policies (UNECE, 2005).

Urban Land: Means land located within an administrative boundary of an urban center (FDRE Proclamation No. 721/2011).

1.9. Organization of the Study

This research consists of five chapters. The first part presents background, significant of the study, objectives of the study, research questions, and limitation and definition of key terms. The second chapter will discuss the key concepts practice and challenges of good governance are used in the research to address the problem in a broader perspective of literature. It develops the theoretical framework of practice and the major challenges of good governance and empirical studies which contain about good governance. The third chapter focuses on research design and methodology. The sampling techniques, sample size, data source and data collection instrument were discussed. In chapter four, critical discussion according to the collecting data and the presentation of all data collects are made. Finally, chapter five summarize the main findings, conclusion part and gives recommendations to assist Bole sub city land development and Management in the future.

Chapter Two

Review of Literature

2.1 Introduction

Is a body of text that aims to review the critical points of current knowledge including substantive findings as well as theoretical and methodological contributions to a particular topic Abdu (2010).This chapter briefly presents literatures related to the concept of good governance. This section reviews the existing theoretical and empirical literature on the practice and challenges of good governance. Specifically, the chapter reviews the guiding theoretical framework relating to the study, their proposition and implication to the study variables. At the end of the chapter presents the conceptual framework for this study and also research gap.

2.2. Concept and Definition of Governance and Good Governance

2.2.1. Concept of Governance

The idea of "governance" is not new. It is previous as human civilization. The awareness of governance have been in the human being nations the time with the intention of the nation learned how to live in one area or society from first to last making decisions and implementations of certain laws, rules and policies in order to live orderly and musically in one environment Muhammad (2015). The term governance is consequent from the Greek term "Kybernan", meaning to guide a ship is loosely used to explain the process by which decisions are made and carried out on behalf of the members of an organization, the stakeholders of a business, or the people of a nation Crouch and Donald (2008). Governance is a wideidea, not simply to describe, a lot of related concepts is attached the matter of democratic system and growth: accepted contribution and development: corruption and development and too the issue of state capability with development (Hilal 2004).

In the same means, governance is the talent of direction-finding society and organization. Governance also involves the connections between structure, procedure and background that decide how authority is exercise, how decision is taken, and how people or other stakeholders have their say. Basically, it is concerning power, associations and responsibility who has the pressure, who decide, how decision makers are held accountable (Azeb.2016).

In addition, UNDP Oslo Center (2009) defines governance is as the process through public strategy decision are made and implement. It is the result of connections, relations and network between the unlike sectors (government, public sector, private sector and civil society) and involve decision negotiation, and different authority family members between stakeholders to determine who gets what, when and how. Also, governance is about processes, not about ends Suchitra (2004). Frequent definitions describe governance as a process by which power is exercised without clearly stating the ends being sought (Abdellatif 2003).

2.2.2 The Concept of Good Governance

According to United Nations (2007).Good Governance is

that the exercises of power through political and institutional processes that square measure clear and responsible, and provides confidence to public contribution The definition of good governance has targeted on what makes organization and policy simpler and economical, in regulate to realize equity, transparency, participation, responsiveness, answerableness, and therefore the rule of law.

Though the government of FDRE has in use important actions to encourage good governance by ratifying a number of international human being right instruments and the FDRE constitution adopt dual government system and accepted most of the internationally accepted human rights conventions since 1991, the process of good governance building is facing serious and complex challenges (Kassahun, 2010).

> *Good Governance is also at the heart of sustainable development and the alleviation of poverty. It is good for economic growth. It augments production inputs, such as labor and capital, and enhances the productivity of those inputs. Good Governance influence the distribution of the benefits of economic growth as income distribution is a crucial factor in transforming growth in to poverty reduction. Governance thus has a dual impact: on growth and its distribution. It can increase growth and improve income equity, reduce poverty and spur advances towards the Millennium Development Goals. (ECA 2005:1).*

According to USAID (2005) good governance is that the capability of state to create up h with associate in nursing economical, effective and responsible public organization procedure. It is characterized by clear, transparent, society participation in call creation, illustration and responsibility by focusing the areas of legislative increase, decentralization and self-ruled governance, opposed corruption, civil military relationships, and rising policy accomplishment.

Good governance may be a major issue in making associate surroundings of calm, constancy and safety within which individuals will follow varied artistic and original activities, making material resource, employment and to promoting human development and assuaging financial condition. However, good governance may be a product of purposeful policies. It needs all the establishments of governance to occupation in accordance with a country's legal provisions of the rule of law, group action of law, cultures and background. So as for the establishments of governance to hold out their functions professionally and with success they have to be in a position with the acceptable capacities. Good governance may be a progress issue with capability building ramifications. According to Suchitra (2004) states that

- Good Governance is predicated upon jointly helpful and loyal contact among government, people and the private limited company.
- Good Governance is a mixture, of contribution, clearness and decision making
- Good Governance is subjective in concept. The values providing the underpinning for governance

2.2.3 Good and Poor Governance

2.2.3.1 Good Governance is predicated on three main factors. There are

- Efficiency refers to the use of resources and involves the connection between inputs and outputs. Akram (1988). Ethiopian Public Administration, Governance and Ethics
- Effectiveness deals with the extent to that the agency achieves the goals or objectives of the organization or program.
- Mobilize civil societies

2.2.3.2. Poor Governance

Poor Governance: manifests itself through collapse to form a transparent separation between public and personal resources: failure to determine expected framework of law and government behavior conductive to growth extreme rules and set of laws, that hinder the performance of markets and provides confidence for rent-seeking priorities incompatible with development, leading to a misdistribution of resources and closely primarily based or non clear higher cognitive process (ADB and ADF 1999).

2.2.4. Principles of good Governance

As UNDP (1997) states that, good governance is transparent, accountable, participatory, efficient and effective, promotes rule of low. Samsudin (2011) described that there are many principles of good governance and most of them are interrelated. According to UNESCAP, good governance has eight major characteristics. They are participatory, consensus oriented, accountable, transparent, responsible, effective and efficient, equitable and inclusive and follow the rule of law. It assures that corruption is minimized, the views of minorities are taken in to account and that the voices of the most vulnerable in society are heard in decision making. It is also responsive to present and future needs of society.

2.2.4.1. Transparency

It means that decisions have taken and their enforcement are done in a manner that follows rules and regulations. Its information is freely available and directly accessible to those who will be affected by such decisions and their enforcement. It also means that enough information is provided in easily and understandable forms. The concept of transparency in administration requires that government decision making process on routine as well as on matters of public importance is made transparent to citizens who may either be affected adversely or benefitted from such decision. Simply, transparency is free flow of information which is made accessible to those concerned. Transparency implies no secrecy about how public services are run, how much they cost, who in charge is and whether or not they are meeting the standards, how decisions are made, how service is rendered or how and when goods and services are delivered.

2.2.4.2 Responsiveness

Good Governance needs that establishments and processes request to serve all customers at intervals a logical time-frame and have mechanisms for raise concepts and giving updates to constituents. Typically a key concern in several societies in transition wherever governments often follow competitive goals, and a scarcity of openness will quickly erode trust in government despite its sensible mechanism. (Azeb2016).

2.2.4.3 Participation

Giving the possibility for all members of society to possess and associate up to now and eventful voice in call that have an effect on them. Participation by men and ladies, ladies and gents could be a cornerstone of excellent governance. Participation will be either direct or through legitimate establishments or legislative body. Even representative kinds of government don't essentially make sure that the considerations of the foremost vulnerable in society area unit taken into reflection in higher cognitive process. Participation mechanisms can give the possibility for clear feedback thus native governments will hear from a broad style of individuals frequently (Mercy Corps 2010).

As World Bank (1999) stated, community participation need not stop at consultation and trends are strengthening towards involving civil society in implementation and service delivery. However, the public participations were not as means of consultation and building vlock to strengthen the relation between the leadership and the community in the sub city.

2.2.4.4. Rule of law

Laws, regulation and codes of conduct ought to be honest and implemented fairly, the laws on human civil rights. One among the effective ways that of tackle weak governance is to appear at the disconnection among establishments at intervals the broader governance scenario as well as the vary of method of the society in common (UNDP 1997).

2.2.4.5. Consensus Oriented

Consensus-oriented means that in a society, anywhere here are as several opinion as there are actor, it is arbitration of different interests to find the best interest of the community. (Ram 2017)

2.2.2.6. Equity and inclusiveness

A society's well-being depends on making certain that everyone its members feel that they need stake in it and don't feel excluded from the thought of society. And as a result would like for to contribute. This needs all teams, however notably the foremost vulnerable, have opportunities to improve or maintain their well being (Azeb 2016).

2.2.4.7. Effectiveness and Efficient

Good governance means processes and establishments manufacture results that meet the requirements of society whereas creating the simplest use of resources at their disposal. The conception of efficiency within the context of good governance additionally covers the property use of natural resources and also the protection of the atmosphere (Mercy Crops 2010)

2.2.4.8. Accountability

Accountability is a key requirement of good governance. Not only governmental institutions but also the private sector and civil society organizations must be accountable to the public and to their institutional stakeholders. Who is accountable to who varies depending on whether decisions or actions taken are internal or external to an organization or institution. In general an organization or an institution is accountable to those who will be affected by its decisions or actions. Accountability cannot be enforced without transparency and the rule of law, elected individuals and organizations charged with a public mandate should be held accountable for specific actions to the public from which they derive their authority. In a narrow sense, accountability focuses on the ability to account for the allocation, use and control of public assets in accordance with legally accepted standards. In a broader sense, it is also concerned with the establishment and enforcement of rules of corporate governance (ADB, 1999)

2.2.5 The concept of Land Administration

2.2.5.1. Definition of Urban Land

Land is defined as a surface of the earth, the materials beneath, the air above and all things fixed to the soil (UNECE, 2005). Since land fulfills many functions and it is used for different purposes and it becomes scares resource as time goes by, the most important issue is planned use and administration of land to ensure sustainable development and best serve the interest of the society (Engida, 2010).

According to Mabogunje (1992) cited by Engida (2010), urban land is a serviced land, a product created by mixed set of public and private agencies. Urban land is the physical base over which any urban system operates. Thus, urban land is considered to be both a resource and a property. As resource, it is the source of income, personal satisfaction, sense of security and social prestige for individuals. On the other hand, as property it is unique possession and the ownership of urban land confers considerably restrained rights of use and profit. Furthermore, according to the FDRE (2011) proclamation enacted for lease holding of urban lands, urban land is defined as the land located within an administrative boundary of an urban center (FDRE, 2011).

2.2.5.2. Main Elements of Land Administration

Land administration is the process of regulating land and property development and the use of land, the gathering of revenues from the land through sales, leasing, and taxation, and the resolving of conflicts concerning the ownership and the use of land (FAO, 2007), ARD,2004, Dake et al 1999). According to, Williamson (2001), Land registration and cadastre is the core component of land administration system to record and archive land information. The recording of land information such as cadastre map must be ensuring the accuracy to guarantee the successful implementation of all the related activities. Williamson added that, if the important land record is missing or incorrect, it will delay the schedule of implementation. And some cases, the absence of land record makes the government hard to identify whether the irregular old possessed land is qualified to involve in the list of beneficiaries.

As suresh (2014) referred Van der Molen et. al. land policy consists of the whole complex of legal and socio economic prescriptions that dictates how the land and the benefits from the land are to be allocated. This definition is integrated form of social, economic and institutional arrangements to relate the access to land and benefit from the proper use of land. Proper use of land is almost impossible without adopting the proper land development instruments, policy and legal prescription. Therefore, land policy is essential for the equitable utilization of the natural resources and proper use of land to improve and reduce the globally increasing haphazard settlement and to reduce the poverty. If we take the land as the economic assets then land policy can be defined as the rules for governing the access to land and distribution of the benefits from the economic asserts (Van der Molen et al. 2008). This definition implies that the land policy can be explained in terms of economic growth, poverty eradication, environmental sustainability and land governance. Good Urban land policy can assist the process of change, include the sustainable land development schemes and endorse the good governance (Docbele, 1982).

2.2.5.3. Land Administration and Land Management

According to ARD (2004), land administration refers to processes of recording and disseminating information about the ownership, value, and use of land and its associated resources. Such processes include the determination of rights and other attributes of the land the survey, description, registration and recording of these rights; and the provision of relevant information in support of land markets. On the other hand, land management, addresses all issues related to the sound and sustainable use of land. It is the process by which the resources of land are put to good use. It covers all activities concerned with the management of land as a resource both from and environmental and an economic perspective (ARD, 2004).

Land Management involves the implementation of fundamental policy decisions about the nature and extent of investments in the land. It involves routine operational decisions made each day by land administrators such as surveyor, valuers and land registers. From an institutional perspective, land management is affected by land policy, the legal framework, issues pertaining to resource management, land administration arrangements and land information management. It entails both government and private initiatives (UNECE, 2005).

2.2.5.4. Overview of the Land Sector in Ethiopia

Land in Ethiopiais a crucial resource with a number of economic, social, political, and philosophical dimensions. Access to land was a key focus of the 1975 revolution that overthrow the imperial regime, after which the Derge regime nationalized all rural land and implemented a program to distribute land to the tillers. In 1991, the transitional government took power after defeating the socialist oriented Military government. Despite the introduction of political and economic changes, land remained public property. The constitution of the Federal Democratic Republic of Ethiopia (FDRE, 1995) unequivocally states that land shall not be individual's property and all land is owned by the state (Plummer, 2012).

The right to ownership of rural land and urban land, as well as of all natural resources is exclusively vested in the state and the peoples of Ethiopia, Land is a common property of the nations, nationalities and peoples of Ethiopia and shall not be subject to sale or to other means of exchange (FDRE, 1995: Article 40:3

"Government has the duty to hold, on behalf of the people, land and other natural resources and to deploy them for their common benefit and development"

According to Plummer (2012), land Administration in Ethiopia is delegated under the constitution to the regions (for rural land) and to city governments and municipalities (for urban land). She added that, Federal oversight of land administration is limited and there is no common system to administer land in urban areas. Urban land is provided through .a lease system, which terms for ranging up to 99 years 2. A perpetual permit system for urban land outside the lease system and 3.Legislation for condominiums. However, the level of informality is high, with some estimates of the informal sector as high as 90% of housing units. Informal settlement has increased in recent years (including the recent phenomena of land grabbing). In Addis Ababa it is estimated that 70-80% of informal settlement is occupied by those who are relatively well-off (Plummer, 2012).

2.2.6. Good Governances and Land Administration

Land governance is about the policies, processes and institutions by which land, property and natural resources are managed. This includes decisions on access to land, land rights, land use, and land development. Land governance is basically about determining and implementing sustainable land policies and establishing a strong relationship between people and land (FIG, 2010: David et al, 2009).

As David et al. (2009) asserted, when land governance is weak, the powerful are able to dominate the completion for scarce land resources. In an extreme form corruption can occur on a grand scale through: state capture". The state can be "captured" by individuals, families, clans, groups or commercial companies who direct public policy for their own benefit. In addition, Bell (2007) noted that, growing insecurity in property rights and high level of corruption in the form of bribery in land administration especially in the developing are the effects of bad land governance. Bell, added that, vulnerable groups such as indigenous farmers, the poor, women and others from the society are most affected by bad land governance. In the public land sector, bad governance is linked to weak institutional frameworks governing security of tenure, inadequate, incoherent and improperly enforced legal provisions, a lack of transparency, accountability, inequity, and lack of institutional irresponsiveness to the plight of land users (FAO,2007 and UN-HABITAT, 2007). Slow and bureaucratic procedures and the high cost of land administration services give rise to bribery, corruption and the misappropriation of public resources (Zakout et al, 2006). Hence, a weak land administration system may be part of more general problems of governance and therefore is linked to low transfer tax collection rates as well as low annual property tax collection rates. This results in poorly resourced local government (UNECE: 2005).

By contrast, when land governance is effective, equitable access to land and security of tenure can contribute to improvements in social, economic and environmental conditions (David et al, 2009). They added that, in cities, effective land management reduces social tensions and promotes economic growth and poverty reduction. When good governance exists, decision making is more transparent and participatory, the rule of law is applied equally to all, and most disputes are resolve before they degenerate in to conflict.

According to David et al (2009), good governance places all decisions on land upon respect for fundamental human rights and ensures that all relevant stakeholders are enabled to effectively participate, particularly women and other vulnerable groups. They added that, the no one stands above the law, and those politicians, officials, land experts and other actors are accountable for their actions. It ensures that rules and procedures are clear, consistent, well understood and applied in a transparent manner. In addition to this, Williamson et al. (2010) noted that, public participation in decision making is highly encouraged and government accountability and the adherence to the rule of law by society are emphasized.

Good governance requires institutional and financial sustainability, policy decisions and administrative action should not compromise the social, economic and environment needs of future generations (David et al, 2009).

To improve the performance of managing urban land governance issues, land administration system is necessary to abide with the principles of good land governance (Liyang, 2014). Land administration is part of the infrastructure that supports good land management. It should be treated as a means to an end, not an end in itself. Land administration provides support for the implementation of land policy and is the basis for good governance. Land administration is concerned with such matters as urban development and maintenance of good land records (UNECE, 2005).

2.3 Empirical Review

2.3.1. Challenges of Administrating Urban Land in Developing Countries

In the past several decades cities in developing world witnessed unprecedented levels of urbanization causing enormous pressure on land, housing and infrastructure. It is estimated that developing countries will undergo a high rise in urbanization from 18% to about 56% and that urban population in Africa and Asia will double between the years 2000 and 2030 (UNFPA2007). UNFPA (2007) stressed that: the future of the cities of the developing countries will develop in the management of urban areas. UNFPA (2007) also stated that, for the expansion of urban areas, particularly in developing countries, shortage of land is not a problem, the problem is dysfunctional land market, misguided regulation and a lack of pro active management policy.

Land Administration system includes process to manage public land, record and register private interests in land, assess land, determine property tax obligations, define land use, and support the development application and approval process. The land sector is particularly susceptible to corruption and rent seeking (Plummer, 2012). As kunte et al, (1998) cited by plummer (2012) expressed that, and is an enormous valuable asset, typically accounting for 30-40% of national wealth in developing countries. The value of land thus creates a significant opportunities for corruption on the part of those with the legal authority to assign, revoke, or restrict rights to (plummer, 2012).

2.3.2. Challenges of Administrating Urban Land in Ethiopia

According to plummer (2012), corruptions in the land sector in Ethiopia is frequently reported in the media and on the internet. Plummer added that, it is estimated that about 15,000 forged titles have been issued in Addis Ababa in the past five years. The housing cooperatives have been the vehicle for massive land grab. She noted also that, the Federal Ethics and Anti corruption Commission (FEACC) indicated that, customer service is the most corrupted sector, followed by the land allocation, national housing, judges and the court system, and the tax system.

Recent studies have been conducted in different parts of the Ethiopia, such as the studies by Girma (2013) in Sebeta: Engda (2010) in Arba Minch: Lulit (2011) in Addis Ababa Berhanu (2014) in Gindo have clearly showed that prevalence of weak land administration and low recording inadequate revenue collection, land conflict and non transparent land allocation. This is assigned to very weak institutional capacity of the respective city and town administration and poor land service delivery. From the above studies, the overall effect of the inefficient urban land administration system in different Ethiopian Cities and Towns results. Inefficient service land allocation, excessive speculation and non transparency in land allocation, uncontrolled informal settlement in urban areas and low standard and unplanned housing (Girma, 2013: Engda (2010) added that there is poor urban land revenue collection. Finally, Lulit (2011): Berhanu (2014) argued that, poor land information system and weak application of good governance principles and lack of coordination of the concerned bodies are seen in urban land administration of the study areas. They added that lack of clear and known service delivery rules and regulation, capacity deficiency, lack of skilled man power and poor land data management were some of the results of the inefficient land administration in their study areas.

Abuse of Power: in the form of malfeasance in office or "official misconduct," is the commission of unlawful act, done in an official capacity, which affects the performance of official duties. Malfeasance in office is often grounds for a cause removal of an elected official by status or recall election. Abuse of power can also mean a person using the power they have for their own personal gain.

Bribery payment is extracted by corrupt officials to perform a free service, to prevent the enforcement of regulations, to secure a favorable decision or to speed up a process, examples include bribes to process land registration, not to enforce building regulations and to secure favorable land use planning decisions (FAO, 2007).

Poor service delivery: The World Bank (1990) also affirms that land administration sector of the sub Saharan countries is one among the most corrupted public sectors and also there is manifestation of poor service delivery which is manifested by service gap.

Nepotism and Favoritism: officials use their influence in favor of family, political associations and friends. Official posts are obtained through purchase or influence, and not through open and competitive recruitment (FAO, 2007).

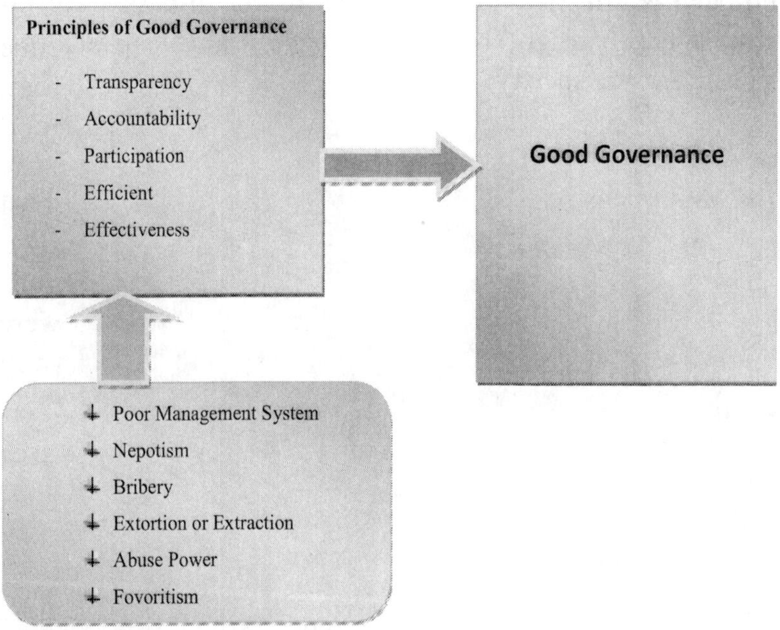

Source: conceptualized by Researcher

Figure 2.1: Conceptual Framework of the Study.

2.4 Research Gap

Good governance is essential to any organizations success. Different research has been conducted in to identifying good governance to enhancing sustainable development for the nation. Even though different researchers conducted different studies concerned on the assessment of challenges & practice of good governance As far as the knowledge of the researcher there is a lack relatively no studies and there is a lot of problem regarding practice and challenges of good governance in Bole sub city Land Development and Management office.

Therefore, the researcher try the lecture from what is complete previous and to fill the gaps investigate of the challenges and practices of good governance in the Land Development and Management office in Bole sub city. Concerned on participation, Transparency, Accountability, efficient & effectiveness. Furthermore, the discussed idea in this research might have its own contribution and too significant for society.

Chapter Three

Research Methodology

Research Methodology is the guidelines in which we approach and perform activities which provide us the principles for organizing, planning, designing and conducting a good research (Haradhan 2017).

This section deals with methodological issues such as, research approach, research type, source of data, data collection instrument, population and sampling, the methods of investigating and analyzing the problem, ethical consideration, validity and reliability of research instrument.

3.1. Description of the Study Area

Addis Ababa is capital city of Ethiopia and the seat of Africa Union, Economic Commission for Africa and number of embassies and Agencies. The City was founded in 1886 by Emperors of Menilik II. Addis Ababa lies between $9^{0}1'48"$ Nand 38^{0} 44' 24" E and has a total area of 540 square kilometers surrounded by Oromia Regional State. The Population of the city is more than 2,739,551 in general and Males account to 1,305,387 and Females account to 1,434,551 in general and Males account to 1,305,387 and Females account 1,434,164 with an annual population growth rate of 2.1% (Central Statistics' Authority (CSA 2007).

Bole is found to the North East of Addis Ababa. The total population of sub city is 328.90 Male: 154,542, Female:

174,358, in addition, it has a total area of 122.08 square kilometer and population density per sq.m: 2,694.1. Oromia regional state bounds it in the Eastern and South Eastern direction, Yeka Sub City to North, in the West Kirkose Sub City and in the South Nifas-Silek Lafito Sub city and Akaki Sub City. (http:/www.addisababa,gov.et/bole)

Accordingly, Bole Sub city have 15 Woreda (Districts). The average annual rain fall is 1180mm (national metrorology of Ethiopia 2010). The average Maximum and Minimum annual temperature are 22.8°C and 10.6°C respectively. The city has loam to clay soil. The socio economic activates are trade, manufacturing industries, hotels and catering, urban agriculture, transport, communication industries, etc.

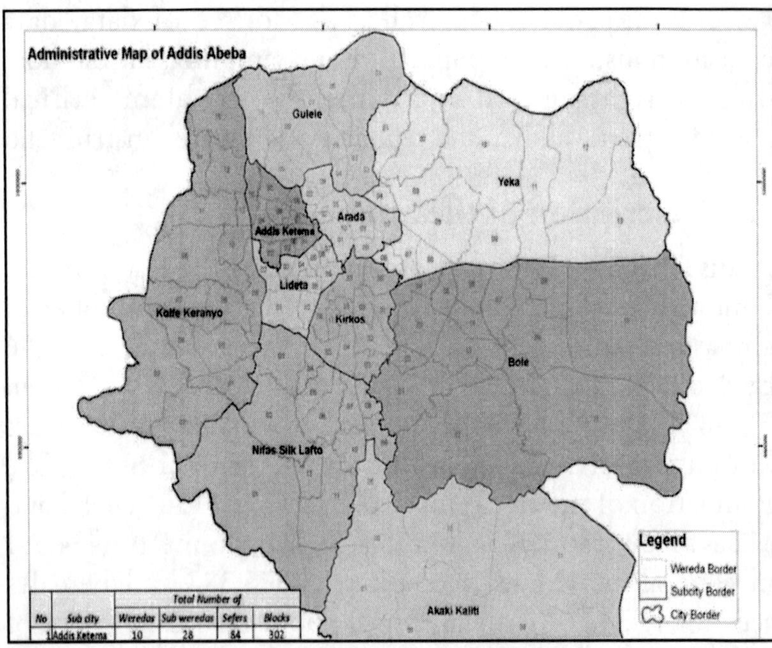

Source: http://www.ilic.gov.et/index.php/en/administrative-boundaries

Fig. 3.1 Map of Addis Ababa city Administration, with its 10 sub- cities and 117 Woredas.

3.2. Research Type

In under taking this study the researcher uses descriptive survey research type was employed. Kothari (2004) states that descriptive research is used to describe characteristics including studies concerning with specific predictions with narration of facts and characteristics of situations. Therefore, the study was employed descriptive survey research design. Because, to describe and identify the facts and information's of good governance in the study area.

3.3. Research Approach

3.3.1. Quantitative Research Approach

To analyze quantitative data the researcher utilizes the statistical package for social sciences software SPSS version 20 and micro soft excel for the data gathered from questionnaires. In analyzing the data descriptive analysis applied. The descriptive analysis used to analyze the frequency and percentage of respondents.

3.3.2. Qualitative Research Approach

Qualitative data is concerned with subjective appraisal of attitudes, opinions and behavior. Research in such a condition is a function of researcher's insights and imitation. Such an approach to research generates results either in non-quantitative form or in the form which are not subjected to rigorous quantitative analysis. Generally, the depth interviews are uses (Kothari, 2004). The information collected from interview triangulated with the quantitative data.

3.4. Population and Sampling Frame

3.4.1. Population and Target Population

Population is collection of persons or objects from which a

sample is selected. A population is a group of individuals, objects, or items from which samples are taken for measurement (Singh 2007).

Target population of the study was Bole sub-city land development and management office have278 professional and administrative civil servant staffs. But the target population of the study has been purposively conducted only on professional public servant officials, this is because the researcher believe that these people have better knowledge and information regarding the issue. The study area concerned on Bole Sub city land development and management office, the target population from service users which was included in the study was only those peoples who visit the office in order to get the service for twenty days. (The researcher to take twenty days purposively)

According to gather information from the office 200 service users visited per day the office for different land related issues. It means 20 days x 200 service users per day =40000 service users as target population for twenty days. Sample population of the study had been 160 of the total population by using simplified formula to determine the sample size developed by Kothari (1990). On the other hand from 278 employee's 153 employees are professional experts, the researcher to take 50 experts purposively for filling the questionnaire. Totally 50+160 =210respondents have been conducted to fill the questionnaire. This is because of resources and time constraints; it is difficult to include all population under the study. Out of 210 questionnaires 190 questionnaires were returned to enter SPSS version 20 for the statistical analysis.

3.4.2 Sampling Frame

Sampling frame is a list of every individual in the population. For the Purpose of this study our sampling frame is employees, leaders and customers of Bole Sub city Land Development and Management office The reason why the researcher selects these organization is because these organization provide services to the large number of the people.

3.5. Sampling Techniques and Sample Size

3.5.1. Sampling Techniques

The Researchers use both probability and non-probability sampling techniques, as stated by Kothari (2004) Probability sampling design, every item of the population has an equal chance of inclusion in the sample but, non-probability sampling is that sampling procedure which does not afford any basis for estimating the probability that each item in the population has of being included in the sample. In non-probability sampling, items for the samples are selected deliberately by the researcher; his choice concerning the items remains supreme. From their rational researcher uses probability sampling for employees and customer (service users) participant. For employee participant use lottery method and for service users selected through systematic sampling technique to survey respondents. In systematic sampling, the sampling frame is first divided into a number of segments called intervals (K) method: k^{th}. = N/n i.e. 4000/ 160= 25. The researcher rolled up a piece of paper with numbers 1 up to 25, randomly 1 number was selected. Thus prospective respondents were selected 1st, 25th, 50th, 75th— until reached 160 respondents. The number of professionals public officials in each department was included in the study and a total of 153 professionals are there and from this 30% (50) identified based on a lottery sampling techniques

The non-probability sampling techniques purposively uses Interviews for head of land development and management office.

3.5.2. Sample Size

For this study, the sample size was determined based on a simplified formula to determine the sample size of the above population the following formula developed .The sampling which are less than 10,000 target populations. According to Kothari (1990), in order to determine the sample size of a population which is less than 10,000, the sample size was calculated using the following formula:

$n = \frac{z^2 * p * q}{d^2}$ Where: n= desired sample size

z= standard normal variable at the required confidence level

p= estimated characteristics of target population

q= 1-p

d= level of statistical significance of target population.

Z= 1.81, p = 0.5, q= 1-p = 0.5, d= 0.07 (in which 93% accuracy is assumed).

Therefore:

$$n = \frac{(1.8)^2 * 0.5 * 0.5}{0.07^2} = \frac{0.819025}{0.0049} = 167$$

Where: *fn*= the desired sample size when the target population is less than 10,000

n= the sample size when the population is less than 10,000

N= target population size

the reason why the researcher use 93 percent confidence level is the researcher assume that this level of confidence is enough and does not bring any effect on the data analysis of the study.

According to Kothari (1990), if N< 10,000 the following formula will be used:

$$fn = \frac{\text{n}}{1 + \frac{\text{n}}{\text{N}}}$$

Where: *fn*= the desired sample size when the target population is less than 10,000

n= the sample size when the population is less than 10,000

N= target population size

Accordingly, n= 167, N= 2000

$$fn = \frac{167}{1 + \frac{167}{4000}} = \frac{167}{1 + 0.04175} = \frac{167}{1.04175} =$$

$$\underline{= 160}$$

Therefore 160 respondents used as a sample from 40000 customers and 50 respondents from 153 professionals to gathered data by using questionnaire.

Table 3.1: Proportional Distribution of Target Population and Sample

Sample Frame		*Total Population*	*Sample Size*	*Sampling Technique*	*Instru-ment*
Staff members under Land Development and Management office	*Offices*				
	Land Tenure and Transition Period Project office	97	97x50/153=31	probability sampling/ Lottery method	
	Land Bank and Transfer office	19	19x50/153=6	probability sampling Lottery method	
	City Plan Commission branch office	25	25x50/153=8	probability sampling/lottery method	Question-naire
	Land Development and Urban Renewal	12	12x50/153=5	probability sampling/ lottery method	
Total		**153**	50		
Customers		4000	160	Probability(systematic sampling)	
Customer + professionals		**4153**	210		
Office Managers		1	1	Purposive (non-probability sampling	Interview

Source: Survey data, 2019.

3.6. Data Source and Data Collection Instruments

In this study, both primary and secondary sources of data will be collected to get the required information because according to (Kumar, 2011) these sources are crucial for the study.

3.6.1. Data Source

3.6.1.1. Primary Sources of Data

Primary sources include finding out first-hand the attitudes of a community. The primary sources of data will be collected from employees and customers by using questionnaires. Applying questionnaire can help the researcher to address large respondents and get much more information about the research.

3.6.1.2 Secondary Sources of Data

Secondary data means data that are already available i.e., they refer to the data which have already been collected and analyzed by someone else. When the researcher utilizes secondary data, then he/she has to look into various sources from where he/she can obtain them. For the purpose of this study, the researcher will use different secondary sources of data such as books from library, published and unpublished reports from study area and the city administration, internet website, and researches conducted on the subject matter.

3.6.2 Data Collection Instruments

3.6.2.1 Questionnaire

According to Kothari (2004), questionnaire help a researcher's to be objective and free from bias .Accordingly, close ended and open ended questionnaires will be presented to the respondents.. The questionnaires will be written in English language and will be translated in to Amharic.

3.6.2.2 Interview

According to Kumar (2011), interviewing is a commonly used method of collecting information from people and also any person-to-person interaction, either face to face or otherwise, between two or more individuals with a specific purpose in mind.

The researcher used semi-structured questions for interview because semi–structured interview items have the advantages of flexibility in which new questions forwarded during interview based on the responses of the interview.

3.7. Method of Data Analysis Method

According to Kothari (2004), data analysis means to find meaning from the data and a process by which the investigator can interpret the data. The analysis of the data will be sorted by the sorting out the data collected according to their categories. Then edited and coded according to the variables. As the first step in analyzing the data for this study, the researcher will read all the information gathered from the completed questionnaire, and the transcription of the interview. The data analysis is divided in to two parts, quantitative and qualitative data. For the quantitative data, use Statistical Package for Social Science (SPSS) version 20 has been used to compute the data collected from the questionnaires.

First, descriptive survey was utilized to calculate the frequencies and percentage of the categories of the researcher required. The result will be presented by using tables that include the frequency and percentage of respondents on each question. The notes of qualitative data (interview) will be categorized and incorporated areas based on similarities of responses and then analyze and discuses through narration and summarization. Finally the result of quantitative analysis can be supported by description of qualitative data that were gathered through interview.

3.8. Reliability and Validity

Reliability (internal consistency) and validity (construct validity) are the statistical criteria used to assess whether the research provides a good measure. They are the two important concepts that should be considered when the researcher designs the instrument. According to Uzunboylu, etal (2016) reliability refers to the consistency of scores or answers from one administration of an instrument to another and from one set of items to another. If an instrument is reliable, it provides consistent result. The term validity refers to the appropriateness, meaningfulness, correctness, and usefulness of any inferences a researcher draws based on data obtained with an instrument (Ibid).

It is the degree to which an instrument measures what it is supposed to measure Atieno, o.p (2009). Reliable measuring instrument does contribute to validity, but a reliable instrument need not be a valid instrument (Xin, S etal, 2013).

Cronbach's alpha is a commonly used test of internal reliability. A cronbach's alpha coefficient varies between 1, denoting perfect internal reliability, and 0, denoting no internal reliability. The figure of 0.75 or more usually is treated as a rule of thumb to denote an accepted level of reliability. To increase the reliability and validity of the study, the researcher will use a mixed method including quantitative and qualitative. Hence, descriptive survey will be taken up to assess the practice and challenges of good governance in land development management in Bole Sub City.

Table 3.2: Results of Reliability Test

Reliability test for employees			*Reliability test for customers*		
Dimensions/ Variables	*Cronbach's Alpha*	*Number of item*	*Dimensions/ Variables*	*Cronbach's Alpha*	*Number of item*
Transparency	0.881	7	Transparency	0.853	7
Accountability	0.896	7	Accountability	0.857	7
Participation	0.918	7	Participation	0.884	7
Efficiency	0,885	9	Efficiency	0.911	9
Effectiveness	0.962	5	Effectiveness	0.884	5
Challenges of good governance implementation	0.946	7	Challenges of good governance implementation	0.919	7

Source: Field Survey, 2019.

According to the results of reliability test, Cronbach's Alpha value of each variable was greater than 0.7. Therefore, it is possible to conclude that all the questions were reliable to measure variables

The **validity** of this study would also checked whenever the researchers had employed pilot test the reliability by taking 15% of respondents questionnaires randomly and by checking the wording and content of the questions.

3.9. Ethical Consideration

Ethical considerations are important, both during data collection and during presentation of data. Therefore essential for the researcher keep in mind the objects of enquiry in a questionnaire, interview and content analysis are human beings. It is very critical to protect them and for them to feel protected at all times. When the respondents agree to be involved in the study, steps taken to ensure that they know exactly what they are agreeing to. The researcher was ensuring that the confidentiality and anonymity of the participants were maintained through the removal of any identified characteristics before widespread dissemination of information. The researcher was clear that the participants name was not used for any other purpose, nor will information be shared that reveals their identity in any way.

Chapter Four

Data Presentation, Analysis and Discussion

4.1. Introduction

This section covers data, analysis and discussion of results of the study. The findings of this study are based in the research objectives which include practice of good governance in order to transparency, accountability, participation, efficiency and effectiveness in land development and management office:, identification of the major challenges for implementation of good governance and identify the solution for the challenges in the study area.

More ever this chapter presents demographic characteristics of respondents, discussion and interpretation.

4.2. Response Rate

In order to attain the objective of the study a total of 210 questionnaires were distributed to the target respondents of the sub city land development and management office. Based on the sampling procedures described in the previous chapters 210 questionnaires were distributed to customers and professional employees of Bole Sub City Land Development and Management Office. From this 91% of the questionnaires were returned and analyzed, Moreover, the researcher conducted interview for leader of the sub city.

4.3 General Background of Respondents from Employee Side

The table below presents the demographic characteristics of 49 sample respondents collected from the field survey including sex, age, educational background, service year and position of respondents.

Table 4.1. General Information of Respondents from Employee Side

Variable	*Categories*	*Frequency*	*Percent*
Gender	Male	28	57.1
	Female	21	42.9
	Total	49	100
Age	20-25	4	8.2
	26-30	13	26.5
	31-35	15	30.6
	36-40	9	18.4
	>41	8	16.3
	Total	49	100
Education Level	<10	-	-
	10-12	-	-
	Level I-IV	-	-
	Diploma	-	-
	First degree	44	89.9
	Masters	5	10.2
	Total	**49**	100
Work Experience	1-2 yrs	6	12.2
	3-4 yrs	6	12.2
	5-6 yrs	11	22.4
	Above 7 yrs	26	53.1
	Total	**49**	100
Position	Senior officer	12	24.4
	Officer	26	53.1
	Process owner	11	22.4
	Total	**49**	100

Source: Field Survey, 2019.

Gender of respondents

As it is depicted in table 4.1, above about the respondents' sex, 28 (57.1%) of the respondents are males while the rest

21 (42.9%) are females. Most of the employees in the organizations are males this shows that male employees are greater than female employees being participant of the organizations. As it is believed that their role in any field of work is high.

Age Distribution of Respondents

With reference the employees age 15 (30.6%) of respondents were 31-35 years old; 13 (26.5%) were 26-30 years old; 9 (18.4%) were between 36-40 years of age, 4 (8.2%) were 20-25 years old 8 (16.3.2%)were above 40 years old . This shows that majority found in age range from 31-35 and active working age.

Education level of Respondents

Regarding the employees level of education, most of the employees (89.8%) of them are first degree holders & (10.2) of them are second degree holders. This is expected to be that the organization has more skilled man power and it is believed to be productive.

Service Year of Respondents

The results show that 53.1% of the respondents had worked with the organization for greater than 7 years; 22.4% of the respondents had worked with the organization between 5 – 6 years, 12.2% of the respondents had worked with the organization between 3-4 years; 12..2% of the respondents between 1-2 years. This shows that majority of respondents service year was greater than 7 years.

Current Position of Respondents

With reference to the position of employees 11(22.4%) of them are core process coordination, 12 (24.4%) of them are Senior Officers, While 26 (53.1%) of them are officers of the organization level. From the table it can observe that majority of the respondents are in expert level which helps the researcher to get more accurate result about good governance, because they know all day to day activities.

4.4 Practice of Good Governance in Land Development and Management Office

In this part the employee's perception on practice of good, based on our questionnaire, the respondents were asked to select the rate that best believed the practice of good governance according to five selected good governance pillars. (Transparency, Accountably, Participation, Efficiency and Effectiveness). Linkert-type scale was used to rate their responses 1- 5 - point scale ranging from 1 = Strongly Disagree to 5 = Strongly Agree.

Table 4.2: Respondents Responseson Transparency

Variable	*Response Rate*	*Frequency*	*Percentage*
In my office there is open and detail service procedure	Strongly disagree	7	14.3
	Disagree	25	51
	Neutral	1	2
	Agree	12	24.5
	Strongly Agree	4	8.2
	Total	**49**	100
In my office there is practice/culture of communicating newly enacted related laws, directives, codes etc. to the public	Strongly disagree	9	18.4
	Disagree	18	36.3
	Neutral	2	4.1
	Agree	14	28.6
	Strongly Agree	6	12.2
	Total	**49**	100
In my office there is enough Information provided on budget is used	Strongly disagree	5	10.2
	Disagree	22	44.9
	Neutral	7	14.3
	Agree	10	20.4
	Strongly Agree	5	10.2
	Total	**49**	100

(*Contd...*)

In my office there is clear information how land is use	Strongly disagree Disagree Neutral Agree Strongly Agree	6 19 3 16 5	12.2 38.8 6.1 32.7 10.2
	Total	**49**	100
In my office there is campaign handling mechanism i.e registration book, suggestion box	Strongly disagree Disagree Neutral Agree Strongly Agree	16 12 3 10 8	32.7 24.5 6.1 20.4 16.3
	Total	**49**	100

Source: Field Survey, 2019.

The above table present that the levels of agreements to contact good governance dimensions in relation to transparency can be seen from five statements. The first question was concerning on open and detail service delivery process in the sub city land development and management office. Accordingly, the majority 25 (51 %) of the respondents disagree, and 12 (24.5%) rated agree. However, 7 (14.3%) of the respondents are strongly disagree to the question. Whereas, 1 (2%) and 4 (8.2. %) of the respondents are neutral and strongly agree respectively. Thus, from this discussion one can conclude that employees of Bole sub city land development and management office have negative perception concerning the open and detail service procedure to service users in land development and management office.

As study result on the above table communicating newly enacted laws, directives, charters, codes... etc to the public, about 18 (36.7%) respondents disagree and 9(18.4) respondents have been strongly disagree, on the contrary the 14(28.6%) respondents agree. However 2(4.1%) of respondents have no answer. Whereas 6(12.2) strongly agree. The respondents respond on open ended question also argued that the leader's commitment to enhance transparent for the public regarding land administration was less. Most of respondents argued that the main causes were lack of commitment and lack of awareness about the role of stockholders on promoting good governance. From the obtained the majority of respondents argued that the sub city land development and management office lacks of awareness in communicating newly enacted laws, directives, charters, codes...etc to the public.

The above study results on the above table on clear information provided how budget is used about 5(10.2) and 22(44.9) also said strongly disagree and disagree respectively, 7(14.3) respondents unable to decide. The rest 10(20.4) and 5(10.2) respondents agree and strongly agree. Based on result of respondents conclude that the office of land development and management had not to give clear information to employees according to budget utilization.

The study indicates about clear land and land relates information to the public at the sub city level, about 6 (.12. %) and 19(38.6%) of the respondents have been chosen strongly disagree and disagree. On the other hand, 16(32.7%) and 5(10.2%) of the respondents have been chosen agree and strongly agree, 3(6.1) respondents have been neutral.. Based on data collected from employees' it concludes that lack of information to give the public on land and land relates issues.

Given the fact that 16(32.7) and 12(24.5) majority of respondents strongly disagree and disagree to complains handling mechanism. , On the other hand 10(20.4) and 8(16.3) agree and strongly agree and 3(6.1) of them respondents undecided. This shows that complains handling mechanism in sub city land development and management office at low level. The respondents respond on open ended question also argued that the leader's commitment to enhance transparent for the public regarding land administration was less. Most of respondents argued that the main causes were lack of commitment and lack of awareness about the role of stockholders on promoting good governance. From the obtained the majority of respondents argued that the sub city land development and management office lacks of transparent in its activity.

Table 4.3: RespondentsResponses on Accountability

Variable	*Response Rate*	*Frequency*	*Percentage*
In my office there is availability of code of conduct for staff	Strongly disagree	7	14..3
	Disagree	21	42.9
	Neutral	-	-
	Agree	12	24.5
	Strongly Agree	8	16.3
	Total	**49**	100
In my officer there is regular evaluation on performance of employees	Strongly disagree	5	10.2
	Disagree	8	16.3
	Neutral	3	6.1
	Agree	24	49
	Strongly Agree	9	18.4
	Total	**49**	100
In my office there is every one questionable for his/her action and decision	Strongly disagree	7	14.3
	Disagree	19	38.7
	Neutral	2	4.1
	Agree	9	18.4
	Strongly Agree	12	24.5
	Total	**49**	100
In my office there is answerability of officials for the effect of their decision on land and land related issues	Strongly disagree	9	18.4
	Disagree	25	51
	Neutral	3	6.1
	Agree	8	16.3
	Strongly Agree	4	8.2
In my office there is consequence reward for good performance	Strongly disagree	7	14.3
	Disagree	27	55.1
	Neutral	1	2
	Agree	11	22.4
	Strongly Agree	3	6.1
	Total	**49**	100

(Contd...)

In my office there is consequence punishment for bad performance	Strongly disagree Disagree Neutral Agree Strongly Agree	22 11 3 7 6	44.9 22.4 6.1 14.3 12.2
	Total	**49**	100
In my office there is culture of exercising authority within legal boundary	Strongly disagree Disagree Neutral Agree Strongly Agree	9 19 4 12 5	18.4 38.8 8.2 24.5 10.2
	Total	**49**	100

Source: Field Survey, 2019.

As far as availability of code of conduct 7(14.3) and 21(42.9%) of the respondents strongly disagree and disagree. Whereas 12(24.5%) and 8(16.3) respondents agree and strongly agree. The result indicates that in the office there is a gap to availability of code of conduct for employees performed their day to day duties and responsibilities.

When we come to mechanism for regular evaluation on performance of employees in the office, 5(10.2) and 8(16.3) respondents strongly disagree and disagree to regular evaluation on employee performance. Whereas 24(49%) and 9 (18.4) respondent agree and strongly agree, 3(6.1%) of them said undecided. This implies that most of the employees argue evaluation and monitoring system on performance in their office.

The result in table above indicated that 7(14.3) and 19(38.7) of the respondents strongly disagree and disagree for every one questionable for his/her action and decision Whereas 9 (18.4 %%) and 12 (24.5%) of respondents agree and strongly agree respectively. On the other hand 2(4.1%) of respondents were not sure for the answer. From this finding it can conclude that employees and leaders in the office are not questionable for decision and action.

Regarding answerability on land and land related issues, majority 9(18.4%) and 25 (51%) respondents strongly disagree and disagree to 8(16.3%) and 4 (8.2%) of respondents agree and strongly agree. But the rest 3(6.1%) of the respondents prefer to neutral in their perception.

In addition to the above respondents response on interview shows that the sub city replied that, even though it has tried to answer for the public question but not enough. From this it can conclude there is a gap to ensure answerability on land and land related issues.

The other point and 27 (55.1%) and 7 (14.3%) respondents disagree and strongly disagree to employees perception on reward for good performance accordingly, Where as 11(22.2%) and 3(6.1%) respondents agree and strongly agree. 1(2%) of them said 'undecided. From the data it concludes that majority of the employees argue that no reward for good performance and punishment for bad performance.

When we come to punishment for bad performance 22(44.9%) and 11 (22.4%) of the respondents considered strongly disagree and disagree, 7 (14.3%) and 6(12.2%) of respondents considered agree and strongly agree 3 (6.1%) respondents were not sure to answer for the question.

Given the fact that culture of exercising authority within legal boundary 9(18.4) and 19 (38.2) of respondents strongly disagree and disagree the organization doesn't have authority within legal boundary. Whereas 12 (24.5%) and 5 (10.2%) agree and strongly agree. The remaining 4 (8.2%) said 'undecided.

Table 4.4: Respondents Responses on Participation

Variable	Response Rate	Frequency	Percentage
In the office there is participate the public by facilitate appealing system and respond promptly	Strongly disagree	10	20.4
	Disagree	15	30.6
	Neutral	1	2.1
	Agree	17	34.7
	Strongly Agree	6	12.2
	Total	**49**	100
In the office there is participating tenure owners on demarcation and adjudication	Strongly disagree	8	16.3
	Disagree	13	26.5
	Neutral	5	10.2
	Agree	20	40.8
	Strongly Agree	3	6.1
	Total	**49**	100
In the office there is participating the customers through commenting	Strongly disagree	7	14.3
	Disagree	16	32.7
	Neutral	2	4.1
	Agree	19	38.8
	Strongly Agree	5	10.2
	Total	**49**	100
In the office there is show genuine interest in solving problem upon request	Strongly disagree	8	16.3
	Disagree	14	28.6
	Neutral	3	6.1
	Agree	18	36.7
	Strongly Agree	6	12.2
	Total	**49**	100
In the office there is Involvement on preparation of plans, problem identification, performance evaluation	Strongly disagree	9	18.4
	Disagree	17	34.7
	Neutral	1	2
	Agree	16	32.7
	Strongly Agree	6	12.2
	Total	**49**	100

Source: Field Survey, 2019.

According to the above table participant response with regard to participate the public by facilitate appealing system and respond promptly 10(20.4%) and 15(30.6%) of the respondents strongly disagree and disagree. 17 (34.7%) and 6 (12.2%) of respondents agree and strongly agree, where as 1 (2%) of respondents neutral to the statements. From this it is possible to understand that employees of the land development and management office recognize the level of citizen participation is judged at weak level.

Our finding in above table shows that when we see participating tenure owners on demarcation and adjudication 8(16.3%) and 13(26.5%) of the respondents strongly disagree and disagree to the statement. However about 20 (40.8%) and 3 (6.1%) of the respondents agree and strongly agree, where as the remaining 5 (10.2%) of respondents are neutral. In interview participants said that community representatives participate on tenure owners on demarcation process. Based on the above finding it can be conclude that participating tenure owners on demarcation and adjudication relatively good.

As faras participating the customers through land service delivery processing commenting 7(14.3%) and 16 (32.7%) of them strongly disagree and disagree, whereas 19 (38.8% and 5 (10.2%) regarding participating the customers through commenting in land service delivery agree and strongly agree. The remaining 2 (4.1%) of the respondents are neutral, from the data observed that there is a gap to participants participate by giving comment for the office.

With regard to genuine interest in solving problems upon request, the majority of respondents 8(16.3%) and 14 (28.6%) of respondents strongly disagree and disagree. On the other hand 18 (36.7% and 6(12.2%) of the respondents agree and strongly agree. But 3 (6.1%) of the respondents were not capable to make a decision on the statement. According to the finding employees of the sub city have motivated to solve public problem.

As a study result on the above table involvement on preparation, implementation and evaluation of plans by land officials to accomplish organizational objectives. It can be observed from table 4.2.3. 9 (18.45%) and 17 (34.7%) of the respondents strongly disagree and disagree. On the other hand 1 (2%) of respondents unable to decide on the question forwarded, Whereas 16(32.7%) and 6 (12.2%) of the respondents agree and strongly agree. From the finding it conclude that the level of employees participates on preparation of plans; problem identification, implementation and evaluation to maintain good governance system were insignificant.

Table 4.5: Respondents Responses on Efficiency

Variable	*Response Rate*	*Frequency*	*Percentage*
In the office there is complete availability of competent personnel	Strongly disagree	4	8.2
	Disagree	17	34.7
	Neutral	2	4.1
	Agree	20	40.8
	Strongly Agree	6	12.2
	Total	**49**	100
In the office there is availability of accurate, integrated and computerized land information	Strongly disagree	4	8.2
	Disagree	17	34.7
	Neutral	3	6.1
	Agree	16	32.7
	Strongly Agree	9	18.4
	Total	**49**	100
In the office there is fast and simple access of land registration	Strongly disagree	7	14.3
	Disagree	22	44.4
	Neutral	3	6.1
	Agree	16	32.7
	Strongly Agree	1	2
	Total	**49**	100
In the office there is ne stop shop service is available	Strongly disagree	8	16.34
	Disagree	18	36.7
	Neutral	1	2
	Agree	17	34.7
	Strongly Agree	5	10.2
	Total	**49**	100
In the office there is standardized service quality	Strongly disagree	7	14.3
	Disagree	16	32.7
	Neutral	2	4.1
	Agree	17	34.7
	Strongly Agree	7	14.3
	Total	**49**	100

(Contd...)

In the office there is efficient utilizing of budget	Strongly disagree	7	14.3
	Disagree	17	34.7
	Neutral	2	4.1
	Agree	16	32.7
	Strongly Agree	7	14.3
	Total	**49**	**100**

Source: Field Survey, 2019.

The information in the above table is concerning complete availability of competent personnel 4 (8.2%) and 17 (34.7%) of respondents strongly disagree and disagree to the statement. Whereas 20 (40.8%) and 6 (12.2%) of respondents agree and strongly agree, but 2 (4.1%) of the respondents were unable to decide on the question forward. According to the finding majority of respondents believe that proper experts set at proper place for ensuring service delivery and employees are competent on their work.

With regard to availability of accurate, integrated and computerized land information 4 (8.2%) and 17 (34.7%) of respondents strongly disagree and disagree to the statement. Whereas 16(32.1%) and 9(18.4%) of the employee respond agree and strongly agree, 3 (6.1%) said undecided to the point. From this it is possible to understand that employees of the office perceived the level of integrated computerized land information to the service users relatively good.

Based on finding of the study regarding too fast and simple access of land registration to the public 7 (14.3%)) and 22 (44.9%) of the respondents strongly disagree and disagree. On the other hand 16 (32.7%) and 1 (2%) of the respondents agree and strongly agree. 3 (6.1%) were remaining neutral. This implies there is a gap to give fast and simple access of land registration on land development and management office of the sub city.

Regarding one stop shop service is available 8 (16.3%) and 18 (36.7%) of respondents strongly disagree and disagree to the statement. On the other hand about 17 (34.7%) and 5 (10.2) agree and strongly agree, where as 1 (2%) of the respondent were remained neutral. This result shows employees of the office doesn't argue on one stop shop.

When we see service quality 7(14.3%) and 16 (32.7) of the respondents strongly disagree and disagree, 17 (34.7% and 7 (14.3%) of the respondents agree and strongly agree, but the rest 1(2%) of the respondent are neutral. From the data it was observed that there is relatively quality service to give for customers at standard time period.

The participant response with regarding to the budget utilization.Shows that 7 (14.3%) and 17(34.7%) of the respondents strongly disagree and disagree, 16 (32.7%) and 7 (14.3%) of the respondents agree and strongly agree. Whereas the remaining 2 (4.1%) of the respondents neutral for the question. This implies that the office was inefficient utilization of resources.

Table 4.6: Respondents Responses on Effectiveness

Variable	*Response Rate*	*Frequency*	*Percentage*
Ability of convince all settlers to comply with redevelopment programs	Strongly disagree	6	12.2
	Disagree	14	28.6
	Neutral	3	6.1
	Agree	19	38.8
	Strongly Agree	7	14.3
	Total	**49**	100
Responsible bodies are competent in managing legal matters	Strongly disagree	11	22.4
	Disagree	15	30.6
	Neutral	3	6.1
	Agree	15	30.6
	Strongly Agree	5	10.2
	Total	**49**	100
The office using information for decision making	Strongly disagree	21	42.9
	Disagree	11	22.4
	Neutral	3	6.1
	Agree	7	14.3
	Strongly Agree	7	14.3
	Total	**49**	100

Source: Field Survey, 2019.

Respondents were asked to their perception on availability of convince all settlers to comply with redevelopment program 6 (12.2%) strongly disagree and 14 (28.6%) of respondents disagree to the statement, 19 (38.8%) and 7 (14.3%) of respondents agree and strongly agree to convince settlers to comply for redevelopment. The significant number of respondents 3 (6.1%) were neutral.

As a study result on the above table shows the majority 11 (22.4%) and 15 (30.6%) of respondents strongly disagree and disagree regarding responsible bodies are competent in managing legal matters, whereas15 (30.6%) and 5 (10.2%) of respondents agree and strongly agree, the remaining 3 (6.1%) was neutral. Based on finding it can conclude that responsible bodies are competent in managing legal matters at poor level.

When we come to level of using information for decision making issue under the study the majority 21(42.9%) and 11(22.4%) of the respondents strongly disagree and disagree to the statement, 7(14.3%) and 7 (14.3%) of the respondents agree and strongly agree to the statements. Whereas the remaining 2 (4.1%) of the respondents neutral for the question. From this data it can conclude that there is a gap to gather information from different direction before decision was made.

4.5. The Major Challenges for the implementation of Good Governance

Table 4.7:Respondents Responseson challenges of good governance

Variable	*Response rate*	*Frequency*	*Percent*
In the office there is poor management system	Strongly disagree	5	10.2
	Disagree	13	26.5
	Neutral	2	4.1
	Agree	21	42.9
	Strongly agree	8	16.3
	Total	**49**	**100**

(Contd...)

In the office there is a problem of Nepotism	Strongly disagree	6	12.2
	Disagree	7	14.3
	Neutral	3	6.1
	Agree	22	44.9
	Strongly agree	11	22.4
	Total	**49**	**100**
In the office there is a problem of Bribery	Strongly disagree	4	12.2
	Disagree	14	28.6
	Neutral	2	4.1
	Agree	15	30.6
	Strongly agree	12	24.5
	Total	**49**	**100**
In the office there is Poor service delivery	Strongly disagree	9	18.4
	Disagree	11	22.4
	Neutral	3	6.1
	Agree	20	40.8
	Strongly agree	6	12.2
	Total	**49**	**100**
There is extortion or extraction	Strongly disagree	5	10.2
	Disagree	13	26.5
	Neutral		
	Agree	25	51
	Strongly agree	6	12.2
	Total	**49**	**100**
In the office there is abuse power	Strongly disagree	5	10.2
	Disagree	13	26.5
	Neutral	2	4
	Agree	22	44.9
	Strongly agree	7	14.3
	Total	**49**	**100**
In the office there is favoritism	Strongly disagree	5	10.2
	Disagree	9	18.4
	Neutral	4	8.2
	Agree	19	38.8
	Strongly agree	12	24.5
	Total	**49**	**100**

Source: Field Survey, 2019.

As shown in the above table 5 (10.2%) of the respondent strongly disagree and 13 (26.5%) disagree with the view of that there was poor management system in the office. Whereas the majority 21 (42.9%) the respondents agreed and 8 (16.3%) strongly agreed. That means 29 (59.2%)

of respondents agreed that poor management system in the office.

The above study results on the above table question raised for respondents was thee is a nepotism in your office 6(12.2%) the respondents strongly disagree and 7 (14.3%) of the respondents disagree with the view of nepotism of the sub city, where as the majority of 22 (44.9%) and 11 (22.4%) of the respondents agree and strongly agreed. This means 33 (67.3%) respondents agreed that there was nepotism in land development and management of the sub city.

The study indicates about bribery 4 (12.2%) of the participant who are strongly disagree, where 14 (28.6%) respondents choose disagree and 2 (4%) are totally unaware to the idea.15 (30.6%) and 12 (24.5%) of the respondents agree and strongly agree for question raised. It implies a bad culture during facilitate service for public.

On the same way the majority of employees give their idea on poor service delivery in the office 9 (18.4) respondents strongly disagree for the information, where as 11 (22.4%) of the respondents disagree for the statements. On the other hand 20 (40.8) and 6 (12.2) employees agree and strongly agree for the idea .3 (6.1%) of respondents are neutral. From the finding it can conclude that the service delivery was poor.

When we come to extortion or extraction in the office 5 (10.2%)and 13 (26.5%) of the employees response are strongly disagree and disagree. On the other hand 25 (51) and 6 (12.2%) of respondents agree and strongly agree.

When we see abuse power the perception of employees 5 (10.2%) and 13 (26.5%) of the respondents strongly disagree and disagree to statement respectively. While about 22 (44.9%) and 7 (14.3%) of respondents agree and strongly agree, about 2 (4.1) employees were unable to decide to the statement.

As a study result on the above table were favoritism between customers 5 (10.2%) and 9 (18.4%)) of respondents strongly disagree and disagree for the statement. Whereas about 19 (38.8%) and 12 (24.5%) of respondents argue and strongly agree that there is favoritism between service providers were 4 (8.2%) unable to decide to the statement.

4.6. General Background of respondents from customer's side

The general back ground of the respondent's analysis mainly focused on four items about. It covers sex of respondents, age of respondents, educational level of respondents and working condition of the respondents. This analysis concerned on 141 respondents only.

Table 4.8 General Information of Respondents from customer side

No	*Description of respondents*	*Variables*	*Frequency*	*Percentage*
1.	Gender	Male	76	53.9
		Female	65	46.1
		Total	**141**	100
2.	Age	20-25	16	11.3
		26-30	36	25.5
		31-35	37	26.2
		36-40	29	20.6
		Above 41	23	16.3
		Total	**141**	100
3.	Educational Level	Below 10	14	9.9
		11-12	18	12.8
		Level I-IV	17	12.1
		Diploma	23	16.3
		First degree	57	40.4
		Masters	12	8.5
		Total	**141**	100
4.	Working condition	Business owner	44	31.2
		Private employee	29	20.6
		Government employee	61	43.3
		Other	7	5
		Total	**141**	100

Source: Field Survey, 2019.

Respondents Gender

When we refer sex, the majority of respondents 76 (53.9%) were male where as 65 (46.1%) are females. Thus, it is possible to say that both males and females are participated on study but the number of males is greater than females.

Respondent Age

With reference the customers age, 37 (26.2 %) of respondents were 31-35 years; 36(25.5%) were 30-36 years; 29 (20.6%) were between 36-40 years of age, 16(11.3%) were 20-25 years 23 (16.3.2%) were above 40 years old. Based on this indication most of the respondents were active working age and easily understand the situation.

Respondents Educational Level

Regarding the customers level of education, 14 (9.9%) of them are below grade 10, 18 (12.8%) are from grade 11—12, 17(12.1%) of the respondents level I-IV, the rest 57 (40.4%) and 12 (8.5%) of the respondents are first degree and masters. This indicated that most of the respondents attend first degree holders and diploma respectively.

Respondents Working Condition

When we seen working condition of the respondents the finding of the above table shows that 61 (43.3%) of the respondents are civil servant in different organization, the next 44 (31.2%) of respondents were business owners, 29 (20.6%) of respondents were private employed, the rest 7 (5%) were unemployed. From this we conclude that most of the respondents civil servant in different governmental organization. Moreover, the second largest were business owners.

4.7. Practice of good governance principles from customer's side

Table 4.9: Respondents Responseson Transparency

Variable	*Response Rate*	*Frequency*	*Percentage*
In the office there is open and detail service procedure	Strongly disagree	48	34
	Disagree	61	43.3
	Neutral	7	5
	Agree	18	12.8
	Strongly Agree	7	5
	Total	**141**	**100**
In the office there is practice/culture of communicating newly enacted related law, directives, codes etc to the public	Strongly disagree	50	35.5
	Disagree	72	51.1
	Neutral	7	5
	Agree	9	6.4
	Strongly Agree	3	2.1
	Total	**141**	**100**
In the office there is enough information provided on how budget is utilized	Strongly disagree	45	31.9
	Disagree	62	44
	Neutral	19	13.5
	Agree	13	9.2
	Strongly Agree	2	1.4
	Total	**141**	**100**
In the office there is clear information how land is use	Strongly disagree	53	37.6
	Disagree	65	46
	Neutral	9	6.4
	Agree	11	7.8
	Strongly Agree	3	2.1
	Total	**141**	**100**
In the office there is Complain handling mechanism	Strongly disagree	65	39
	Disagree	47	33.3
	Neutral	6	4.3
	Agree	28	19.9
	Strongly Agree	5	3.5
	Total	**141**	**100**

Source: Field Survey, 2019.

As shown in the above table regarding open and detail service for customers, out of the respondent 48 (34%) and 61 (43.3%) of the respondents strongly disagree and disagree on the case of open and detail service procedures for public, in contrast to this point 18 (12.8%) and 7(5%) of the respondents agree and strongly agree. In the case of open and detail service procedures for public. While 7 (5%) of the respondents were undecided.

The result of survey interview indicated that decisions taken and their enforcement are done in approach that follows rules and regulations. Its information is freely available and directly accessible to those who will be affected by such decisions and their enforcement. It also means that enough information is provided in easily and understandable forms.

Regarding culture of communicating newly enacted related laws, directives, codes etc to the public. Based on respondents response, the majority of the respondents 50 (35.5%) and 72 (51.1%) strongly disagree and disagree. On the other hand 9 (6.4%) and 3 (2.1%) of the respondents agree and strongly agree. The remaining respondents 5 (5%) were un decided to the question that the office communicating newly enacted laws, directives, codes, etc to the service users. From the above information it can be conclude that 112(86.6%) respondents disagree on the idea Where as 12 (8.3%) of the respondents agree to the statements.

According to respondents in interview said that the practice of newly enacted rules and different directives transparent for customers on time were low in sub city level in land development and management office. Because the leaders and the employees of the sub city do not aware the customers when newly enacted different rules and procedures. Based on this their customers don't know their right and responsibilities.

Regarding to budget utilization 45 (31.9%) and 62 (44%) of the respondents strongly disagree and disagree. Where as 13 (9.2%) and 2 (1.4%) of the respondents agree and strongly agree, the remaining 19 (13.5%) undecided to the question. Based on the above discussion it can be concluding that there no information to the public on how budget were used.

According to the above table 54 (38.3%) and 61(43.3%) of the respondents strongly disagree and disagree to clear information how utilized land for their customers, on the other hand 15 (10.6%) and 3 (2.1) of the respondents agree and strongly agree, whereas 8 (5.7%) of them said undecided to the idea. Additionally the respondent's response on open ended question regarding the idea they agreed the leaders of the sub city lack of courage to disclose the report (utilization of land) because of their poor performance in different activities and corruption behavior.

The other question regarding transparency was complains handling mechanism. 65((39) and 47(33.3) respondents have been answered strongly disagree and disagree. On the other hand 28 (19.9%) and 5 (3.5) agree and strongly agree and 6(54.3) of respondents unable to decide. This shows that the information was less accessible to the citizen. Besides response on open ended question shows the involvement of all concerned bodies in the sub city land development and management was less. Even if the problem raised by service users were not solved on time. Response of interview respondents also constructs the idea of customers that involvements of stock holders were not adequate enough. This shows that the leader of the sub city was less responsiveness.

The study sought to determine the respondents with above statement relating to the availability of code of conduct, from the findings that majority of the respondents 37(26.2%) and 70(49.6%) strongly disagree and disagree. Whereas 22(15.2%) and 5(3.5%) respondents agree and strongly agree.

Table 4.10: Respondents Responses on Accountability

Variable	*Response Rate*	*Frequency*	*Percentage*
In the office there is availability of code of conduct for staff	Strongly disagree	37	26.2
	Disagree	70	49.6
	Neutral	7	5
	Agree	22	15.2
	Strongly Agree	5	3.5
	Total	**141**	100
In the office there is regular evaluation on performance of employees	Strongly disagree	44	31.2
	Disagree	58	41.1
	Neutral	15	10.6
	Agree	19	13.5
	Strongly Agree	5	3.5
	Total	**141**	100
In the office every one questionable for his/her action and decision	Strongly disagree	50	35.5
	Disagree	55	39
	Neutral	6	4.3
	Agree	23	16.3
	Strongly Agree	7	5
	Total	**141**	100
In the office there is answerability of officials for the effect of their decision on land and land related issues	Strongly disagree	52	36.9
	Disagree	62	44
	Neutral	12	8.5
	Agree	10	7.1
	Strongly Agree	5	3.5
	Total	**141**	100
In the office there is consequence reward for good performance	Strongly disagree	54	38.3
	Disagree	60	42.6
	Neutral	15	10.6
	Agree	10	7.1
	Strongly Agree	2	1.4
	Total	**141**	100
In the office consequence punishment for bad performance	Strongly disagree	50	35.5
	Disagree	67	47.5
	Neutral	14	9.3
	Agree	8	5.7
	Strongly Agree	2	1.4
	Total	**141**	100
In the office there is culture of exercising authority within legal boundary	Strongly disagree	51	36.2
	Disagree	65	46.1
	Neutral	15	10.6
	Agree	6	4.3
	Strongly Agree	4	2.8
	Total	**141**	100

Source: Field Survey, 2019

Based on these findings the result indicates that there is no availability of code of conduct for employees performed their day to day duties and responsibilities.

As indicated in table above 44 (31.2%) and 58 (41.1%) of respondents strongly disagree and disagree that the practice of mechanism for regular evaluation on performance of employees in the office. Whereas 19 (13.5%) and 5(3.5) agree and strongly agree for the statements. It also 15(10.6%) of the respondents were not sure whether there is regular monitoring and evaluation system in the sub city land development and management office to evaluate the service delivery. Responses on interview also indicated the mechanism of regular evaluation was rarely practiced.

The other point every one asked for her/his action and decision for ensuring service delivery the majority of respondents 50(35.5) and 55(39) strongly disagree and disagree to the statement respectively, that all employees and leaders in the office have no questionable for her/her decision.. Whereas 23 (16.3%) and 7 (5 %) of respondents agree and strongly agree to the statement respectively. On the other hand 6(4.3%) respondents were not sure for the answer. This implies that the majority of respondents conclude the practice of accountable was poor and very poor in the sub city land development and management office.

The other question asked whether there is answerability of officials for the effect of their decision on land and land related issues 52 (39.9%) and 62 (44%) respondents strongly disagree and disagree, on the other hand 10 (7%) and 5 3.5%) respondents agree and strongly agree. The remaining 12 (8.5%) of the respondents prefer to neutral in their perception.

Regarding the question consequence reward for good performance 60 (42.6%) and 54 (38.3%) of respondents disagree and strongly disagree, 10 (7.1%) and 2 (1.4%) respondents response agree and strongly agree Whereas 15 (10.6 %) of the respondents were not sure to answer the question. As a result most of the respondents responded shows that there is a gap to implement reward system to motivate employees.

When we come to punishment for bad performance 67 (47.5%) and 50 (35.5%) of the respondents considered disagree and strongly disagree, 8 (5.7%) and 2 (1.4%) of respondents considered agree and strongly agree 14 (9.3%) respondents were not sure to answer for the question. Additionally responses on open ended question show that imposed on employees who committed good governance is simple and does not give lesson to others. The simplicity of the punishment itself encourages others to commit good governance.

The last question was asked whether there is culture of exercising authority within legal boundary, it can observed from above table 51(36.2%) and 65 (46.1%) of respondents strongly disagree and disagree respectively. Whereas 6(4.3%) and 4 (2.8%) agree and strongly agree. The remaining 15 (10.6%) prefer to neutral in their perception. In addition to this the respondents in interview believed that there is a gap to exercising authority within legal boundary.

Table 4.11: Respondents Response on Participation

Variable	*Response Rate*	*Frequency*	*Percentage*
In the office there is participate the public by facilitate appealing system and respond promptly	Strongly disagree	52	36.9
	Disagree	63	44.7
	Neutral	7	5
	Agree	17	12.1
	Strongly Agree	2	1.4
	Total	**141**	100
In the office there is participating tenure owners on demarcation and adjudication	Strongly disagree	52	36.9
	Disagree	55	39
	Neutral	8	5.7
	Agree	23	16.3
	Strongly Agree	3	2.1
	Total	**141**	100

(Contd...)

In the office there is participating the customers through commenting	Strongly disagree Disagree Neutral Agree Strongly Agree	5 20 5 48 63	3.5 14.2 3.5 34 47.7
	Total	**141**	100
In the office there is show genuine interest in solving problems upon request	Strongly disagree Disagree Neutral Agree Strongly Agree	44 73 2 18 4	31.2 51.8 1.4 12.8 2.8
	Total	**141**	100
In the office there is involvement on preparation of plans and evaluation	Strongly disagree Disagree Neutral Agree Strongly Agree	65 12 12 52 -	46.1 8.5 8.5 39.19 -
	Total	**141**	100

Source: Field Survey, 2019.

As indicated in table 4.11.Regarding to participating the public by facilitating appealing system and respond prompt the majority 52 (36.9. %) and 63 (44.7%) of the respondents strongly disagree and disagree to the statement. 17 (12.1%) and 2 (1.4%) of the respondents agree and strongly agree, whereas, 7 (5%) neutral to the question. From this it is possible to understand that customers of the land development and management office satisfaction level of public participation at weak level.

Regard to. Participating tenure owners on demarcation and adjudication 52(36.9%) and 55(39%) of the respondents strongly disagree and disagree to the statement. However about 23 (16.3%) and 3 (2.1%) of the respondents agree and strongly agree, where as the remaining 8 (5.7%) of respondents are neutral. Based on the above finding it is possible to conclude that the level of participating tenure owners on demarcation and adjudication of adjudication in the sub city was very low.

Regard to participating the customers through commenting in land service delivery process, 5(3.5%) and 20 (14.2%) strongly disagree and disagree, 48 (34%) and 63 (47.7%) of respondents agree and strongly agree. The remaining 5 (3.5%) of the respondents are neutral, from the data observed the majority of the respondents agree to the idea and also the researcher observed from secondary data there is a comment receiving mechanism that is notebook, suggestion box, and also the response of key informant interview show that in our office there is organized comment receiving mechanism but most of the customers not interested to write response on how to the service facilitated.

With regard to question show genuine interest in solving problems upon request, the majority of respondents 14(31.7%) and 73 (51.8%) of respondents strongly disagree and disagree. On the other hand 18 (12.8%) and 4(2.8%) of the respondents agree and strongly agree. But 2 (1.4%) of the respondents were unable to decided. Based on this the majority of service users not satisfied due to employee's lack of attention to solve their problem.

The other important question concerned on service users involvement on preparation of planning, problem identification, implementation, controlling and evaluation illegal land development and informal settlement the majority of respondents 65 (46.1%) and 12 (8.5%) strongly disagree and disagree. On the other hand 52 (39.19%) agree 12 (8.5%) unable to decide on the question forwarded.

The researcher also conducted with interview, the level of customer's participation specially in planning, problem identification, controlling and performance evaluation were poor. From this point of view it can conclude the sub city land development and management office shortage of service user participation during formulation, implementation and evaluation of different plans, policies, etc.

Table 4.12: Respondents Response on Efficiency

Variable	*Response Rate*	*Frequency*	*Percentage*
In the office there is complete availability of competent personnel	Strongly disagree	45	31.9
	Disagree	65	46.1
	Neutral	7	5
	Agree	18	12.3
	Strongly Agree	6	4.3
	Total	**141**	100
In the office there is availability of accurate, integrated and computerized land information	Strongly disagree	49	34.8
	Disagree	57	47.5
	Neutral	1	0.7
	Agree	19	13.5
	Strongly Agree	5	3.5
	Total	**141**	100
In the office there is fast and simple access of land registration	Strongly disagree	48	34
	Disagree	67	47
	Neutral	8	5.2
	Agree	14	9.3
	Strongly Agree	4	2.8
	Total	**141**	100
In the office there is one stop shop service is available	Strongly disagree	57	40.4
	Disagree	60	42.6
	Neutral	8	5.7
	Agree	15	10.6
	Strongly Agree	1	1.7
	Total	**141**	100
In the office there is standardized service quality for customers	Strongly disagree	50	35.5
	Disagree	73	51.8
	Neutral	6	4.3
	Agree	9	6.1
	Strongly Agree	3	2.1
	Total	**141**	100
In the office there is efficient utilizing of budget	Strongly disagree	54	38.3
	Disagree	72	36.9.
	Neutral	22	15.6
	Agree	12	8.5
	Strongly Agree	1	0.7
	Total	**141**	100

Source: Field Survey, 2019.

The result of table 4.12, Indicate that respondents strongly disagree and disagree on complete availability of competent personnel 45 (31.9%) and 65 (46.1. %) respectively. Whereas 18 (12.5%) and 6 (4.3%) of respondents agree and strongly agree, but 7(5%) of the respondents were unable to decide on the question forward. According to the finding Majority of respondents believe that there is incompetency employees in the office.

With regard to the question Availability of accurate, integrated and computerized land information 49 (34.8%) and 57 (47.57%) of the respondents strongly disagree and disagree to the statement. 19(13.5%) and 5(3.5%) of the respondents agree and strongly agree to the statement. About1 few of the respondents were neutral to the statement. From this it is possible to know that customers argue that the existing practice of documentation and registration arrangement was weak. Based on this the sub city without appropriate land registration and documentation system cannot deliver service efficiently and effectively.

The other question on table above regarding too fast and simple access of land registration to the public 48 (34%)) and 65 (46.1%) of the respondents strongly disagree and disagree to the question. On the other hand 14 (9.3%) and 4 (2.8%) of the respondents agree and strongly agree. 8 (5.2%) were remaining neutral. This implies there is a gap to get fast and simple access of land registration.

Regarding one stop shop service is available 57(40.4% and 60 (42.6%) of respondents strongly disagree and disagree to the statement. On the other hand about 15 (10.6%) and 1(0.7%) agree and strongly agree, where as 8 (5.72%) of the respondent were remained neutral. This result shows that service users do not get service at one place; this implies impact on service users for additional cost and wastage of time.

According to the table above standard service quality more than half of the respondents 50 (35.5%) and 73 (51.8) strongly disagree and disagree, 9 (6.4% and 3 (2.1%) of the respondents agree and strongly agree, the remaining 6 (4.3%) of the respondent are no answer for the question. According to interview respondent and secondary data observed that the office put citizen charter, at open place, clear and open written document for quality of service delivery concerned on each activity. But for the period of field survey it was observed that there is still practical problem when it comes to performance.

The participant response with regarding budget utilization the above table shows that 54 (38.3%) and 72 (36.9%) of the respondents strongly disagree and disagree to the statement, 12(8.5%) and 1 (0.7%) of the respondents agree and strongly. agree to the statements. Whereas the remaining 22 (15.6%) of the respondents neutral for the question. This implies that the office was inefficient utilization of budget.

Table 4.13: Respondents Responses on Effectiveness

Variable	*Response Rate*	*Frequency*	*Percentage*
In the office there is Ability of convince all settlers to comply with redevelopment programs	Strongly disagree	56	39.2
	Disagree	57	40.4
	Neutral	14	9.9
	Agree	10	7.1
	Strongly Agree	3	2.1
	Total	**141**	100
In the office there is responsible bodies are competent in managing legal matters	Strongly disagree	51	36.2
	Disagree	61	43.3
	Neutral	9	6.4
	Agree	16	11.3
	Strongly Agree	4	2.8
	Total	**141**	100
In the office there is different information using for decision making	Strongly disagree	45	31.9
	Disagree	60	42.6
	Neutral	12	8.2
	Agree	15	10.6
	Strongly Agree	9	6.4
	Total	**141**	100

Source: Field Survey, 2019.

The response of the first variable revealed that the large majority 56 (39.2%) and 57 (40.4%) of respondents strongly disagree and disagree that there is lack of convince all settlers to comply with redevelopment programs. On the other hand 10 (7.1%) and 3 (2.1%) of the respondents believed that in the office there is ability of convince all settlers to comply with redevelopment programs. However, 14 (9.9%) of respondents were not willing to give neither positive nor negative response on the issue. Besides, surprisingly a large number 113 (79.6%) agreed that providing ability of convince all settlers to comply with redevelopment were very low it rather use their power.

When we look at the above table shows that responsible bodies are competent in managing legal matters the majority 51 (36.2%) and 61 (43.3%) of the respondents claimed that responsible bodies are competent in managing legal matters were very low, On the other hand 16 (6.4%) and 4 (2.8%) of the respondents agree and strongly agree for the statement respectively. Whereas9 (6.4%) of the respondents preferred to be abstainers and they did not give response.

On the hand respondents indicated their view on the variables that are related to using information for decision making issue under the study. As a result the majority 45(31.9%) and 60(42.6%) of the respondents strongly disagree and disagree to the statement, 15(10.6%) and 9(6.4%) of the respondents agree and strongly agree to the statements. Whereas the remaining 12 (8.2%) of the respondents neutral for the question. From this data it can conclude that there is a gap to gather information from stockholders at different level.

4.8 The Major Challenges for the implementation of Good Governance from customer side

Table 4.14, Implies discusses the findings of the study in relation to the challenges a of good governance from perspective of customers in land development and management office of Bole Sub city.

Table 4.14: Respondents Response of Challenges of good governance form customers side

Variable	*Response rate*	*Frequency*	*Percent*
In the office there is poor management system	Strongly disagree	14	9.9
	Disagree	15	10.6
	Neutral	3	2.1
	Agree	68	48.2
	Strongly agree	41	29.1
	Total	**141**	**100**
In the office there is a problem of Nepotism	Strongly disagree	7	5
	Disagree	11	7.8
	Neutral	7	5
	Agree	66	46.8
	Strongly agree	50	35.5
	Total	**141**	**100**
In the office there is a problem of Bribery	Strongly disagree	10	7.1
	Disagree	8	5.7
	Neutral	13	9.2
	Agree	63	44.7
	Strongly agree	47	33.3
	Total	**141**	**100**
In the office there is Poor service delivery	Strongly disagree	8	5.7
	Disagree	16	11.3
	Neutral	3	2.1
	Agree	66	46.8
	Strongly agree	48	34
	Total	**141**	**100**
In the office there is extortion or extraction	Strongly disagree	8	5.7
	Disagree	11	7.8
	Neutral	9	6.4
	Agree	67	47.5
	Strongly agree	46	32.6
	Total	**141**	**100**
In the office there is abuse power	Strongly disagree	7	5
	Disagree	9	6.4
	Neutral	9	6.4
	Agree	62	44
	Strongly agree	54	38.3
	Total	**141**	**100**

(Contd...)

In the office there is favoritism	Strongly disagree	7	5
	Disagree	12	8.5
	Neutral	5	3.5
	Agree	62	44
	Strongly agree	55	39
	Total	**141**	100

Source: Field Survey, 2019.

As shown in the above table 14 (9.9%) of the respondent strongly disagree and 15 (10.6%) disagree with the view of that there was poor management system in the office. Whereas the majority 68 (48.2%) the respondents agreed and 41 (29.1%) strongly agreed. That means 109(77.3%) of respondents agreed that there was poor management system in the office. Thus from the majority's respondents response it can conclude poor management system was one of the challenge for ensuring good governance.

The other point raised for respondents was thee is a nepotism in your office 7(5%) the respondents strongly disagree and 11 (7.5%) of the respondents disagree with the view of Nepotism of the sub city, where as the majority of 66 (46.5%) and 50 (35.5%) of the respondents agree and strongly agreed. The remaining 7 (5%) of the respondents were no answer for the statements. From the finding it can conclude that there was no equal access to get service from the office, there was discrimination.

As table above revels that relatively the majority 63 (44.2%) and 47 (33.3%) customers confirmed that bribery was practiced the level of management and employees respectively. However, 10 (7.1%) and 8 (5.6%) of the respondents strongly disagree and disagree, where as 13 (9.2%) of the respondents was neutral.

On the same way service users give their idea on poor service delivery in the office 8(5.7) respondents strongly disagree for the information, where as 16 (11.3%) of the respondents disagree for the statements. On the other hand 66 (46.8) and 648(34%) of respondents agree and strongly agree for the statements.3 (2.1%) of respondents are neutral. Based on result of finding service users were dissatisfied regarding the performance of land officials in their service delivery for different requests.

The other question raised for respondents, there are Extortion or extraction in the office 8(5.7%)and 11 (7.8%) of the employees response are strongly disagree and disagree. On the other hand 65 (47.5%) and 46 (32.6%) of respondents agree and strongly agree for the statements.

On the statement of abuse power the perception of respondents 7 (5%) and 12 (8.5%) of the respondents strongly disagree and disagree to statement respectively. While about 62 (44.%) and 55 (39%) of respondents agree and strongly agree, about 5 (3.5) of respondents were unable to decide to the statement.

The Other important question were favoritism between customers 7(5%) and 12 (8.5%)) of respondents strongly disagree and disagree for the statement. Whereas about 62(44%) and 55(39%) of respondents argue that there is favoritism between service providers. were 5(3.5%) unable to decide to the statement.

From the above point the majority of the respondent's response shows that poor management system, abuse power, Nepotism and extortion or extraction the major challenges of good governance in sub city.

Based on response of qualitative data from open ended questionnaire, respondents said that the perception of customers in realizing good governance is low. They also believed that they can get service only when they give money to managers and civil servant. They do not know their right and responsibilities. This implies due to low perception of customers and lack of getting the opportunity to participate in planning, implementation and evaluation period of land and related issues. Besides this there is no accessibility of information about rules, regulation procedures to get better service from the office.

Lack of qualified man power also hinder for implementation of good governance This is because civil servant who are employed in land development and management office do not have the required knowledge and attitude that can help them to properly realize good governance.

In addition respondents respond on open ended question for challenges of good governance implementation that lack of competency leader ship, commitment of leader, motivation of leader, absence democratic leader ship style. And leaders have not the necessary knowledge, skill and attitude.

Chapter Five

Summary of Finding, Conclusion and Recommendation

5.1 Summary of Findings

5.1.1 Findings Related with Practice of Good Governance

This chapter summarizes the objectives of the study based on the major findings and conclusions. It also discusses the managerial and theoretical implications of the study, and makes recommendation for further research.

The purpose of the study was to assess practice and challenges of Good Governance in Bole sub city Land Development and Management sector. Based on the analysis of data and discussion of results. The followings are the summary of major findings of this study.

The result of the analysis on practices of good governance based on transparency shows that; 78% of the result of study indicates disagree to culture of communicating newly enacted related laws, directives, codes etc to the public a great factor, 75% indicates gap on clear and enough information on how land use is a great factor, 74% gap of open and detail service procedures as great factors, 73% complain handling mechanism plays great role, 70.5% indicates enough information on budget utilization is a great factor, plays a major role in the practice of good governance in order to transparency. The above finding shows that the major factors in the practice of transparency process were; culture of communicating newly enacted related laws, directives, codes etc. to the public, lack of clear and enough information on how land was use, open and detail service procedures, complaign handling mechanism, budget utilization, were the major problems of practicing good governance in the sector. According to (UNESCAP: Rojina, 2010) Transparency means that decisions taken and their enforcement are done in a manner that follows rules and regulations. Its information is freely available and directly accessible to those who will be affected by such decisions and their enforcement. In general the result shows that information provided by the land development and management office was very low. In supporting of this idea the leaders participating in interview said that there is lack of transparency in the office.

Although according to UNDP (2012) noted that to applying of political and managerial power at each and every one levels to mange a country's associations.

According to ADB (1999) Accountability is a key requirement of good governance. Not only governmental institutions but also the private sector and civil society organizations must be accountable to the public and to their institutional stakeholders. Who is accountable to who varies depending on whether decisions or actions taken are internal or external to an organization or institution. In general an organization or an institution is accountable to those who will be affected by its decisions or actions. From this point of view 79% of the result of the study indicate answerability of officials for the effect of their decision and action were the major factor, 74% of the result of the study indicate that consequence of reward for good performance play great role, 71% availability of code of conduct for employess as great factor 53% of the result of the study shows regular evaluation on performance were the major problems of accountability in the sector.

Based on the analysis report on participation in good governance process indicates that, 74% has a problem with participate the public by facilitate appealing system and respond promptly, 73% indicates problem with genuine interest in solving public problem on request, 67.4% indicates participating tenure owners on demarcation and adjudication of land related issues, 52.4% has a problem with involvement stockholders on plan preparation, implementation and evaluation period, 25%% shows that problems with, participating the customers through commenting were the major problems in participation activities in the organization. As World Bank (1999) stated, community participation need not stop at consultation and trends are strengthening towards involving civil society in implementation and service delivery. However, the public participations were not as means of consultation and building block to strengthen the relation between the leadership and the community in the sub city.

Based on the analysis report on efficiency in good governance process indicates that, 79% has a problem with efficient utilization of budget, 77% indicates problem to give standard service to the public, 76% indicates problem to give fast and simple access of land registration, 75% has a problem with one stop shop service availability, 70% shows that problems with, complete availability of competent personnel, 67% indicated problem with availability, of accurate integrated and computerized land information. were the major problems in efficiency in the organization. According to Mercy Crops, (2010) Good governance means processes and establishments manufacture results that meet the requirements of society whereas creating the simplest use of resources at their disposal. The conception of efficiency within the context of good governance additionally covers the property use of resources and also the protection of the atmosphere.

With regard to effectiveness 75% indicates problem with responsible bodies are competent in managing legal matters, 72% has a problem of gathering different information for decision making, 70 indicates problem with ablity of convince all settlers to comply with redevelopment program.

5.1.2 Findings Related with Challenges of Good Governance

The results of the study indicates that; there were challenges like poor management system Nepotism, Bribery, Favoritism, Extraction abuse power poor service delivery in good governance process. The major challenge of good governance based on the finding shows that the majority 78.4% of responses shows that there were nepotism in the organization; 77.8% of the result indicates that there is favouritism problem; around 76% of the result shows that there is abuse power in their organization, 75% problem faced on extraction and 73% shows there were poor service delivery, 72.6% shows poor management system and 72% says bribery in the implementation good governance in the organization.

The questioner analysis regarding the outcome of the interview and the results of the process, leaders did not give attention for the implementation of good governance, lack of commitment, communication gap. Although there was a problem with the work ethics, there was a shortage of skilled man power, lack of continuous support and supervision, lack of accountability, lack of prior planning, and poor coordination with the community. Were the major challenges on implementation of good governance.

5.2. Conclusion

To ensure good governance in land development and management office of the sub city, the importance of effective implementation of good governance principle is unquestionable. The general purpose of the study was to assess the implementation of good governance in land development and management office of the sub city from the principles transparency, accountability, participation, efficiency and effectiveness perspective. And identify the major challenges faced on implementation of good governance.

The majority of respondents express their greatest dissatisfaction with the land administration in order to transparent. This is because there is discrimination among individuals in service delivery in effective service delivery, inconsistent land laws non transparent decision making, lack of compiling handling mechanism, lack giving enough information to the public how land use or administrated, it is a gap to inform budget utilization and lack of culture of communication newly enacted rules to stockholders.

The study shows that lack of participation there is unaccountable in land development and management in the study area, It shows poor questioning mechanism and negligence to take corrective measures for wrong doing, poor reward system for good performance, lack of regular monitoring and evaluation mechanism, lack of commitment, lack of answerability of officials for the effect of their decision, From the finding it can conclude that commitment of leader is at low level. Additionally there is a weak structure that makes the employees and officials answerable for the effect of their decision and action.

The finding shows that there is a gap public participation in land administration. By facilitate appealing system and respond promptly, participating tenure owners on demarcation and adjudication, participate stockholders on plan preparation implementation and evaluation.

Regarding the efficiency and effectiveness, the study shows that service users were dissatisfied on the availability of accurate, integrated and computerized land information, in their service delivery for different needs. In addition, providing service as per the service delivery standards in the office was very low. There was also bureaucratic delay and drawn out process in the service provision and that was highly hurting the service users. Service users claim that the existing practices of fast and simple access of land documentation and registration system was very weak; the land registration and property transfer procedure was boring. There was a gap to convince all settlers to comply with redevelopment. The study exposed that there was no customer service delivery under one stop shop and the process was long and have several steps. As a result the procedure is very boring and impact on fast service delivery and implementation of good governance in order to achieve organizational objectives and goals. The study also identified lack of competent personnel in the land delivery process.

Generally, there is a lack of good governance in land development and management office of Sub City from good governance dimension as transparency accountability, participation, efficiency and effectiveness. It can, conclude that that governance of the sub city needs to build a system that will promote transparency, accountability participation, efficiency and effectiveness In compliance with the above weaknesses to bringing good governance to the desired scale of excellence in the sub-city.

The major challenges faced was poor management system, Nepotism, Bribery, Poor service delivery, Extortion, abuse power, lack of committed man power, lack of customer handling mechanism, lack of integration.

5.3. Recommendation

Based on finding of the study, the following recommendations are given which are helpful for the land development and management office of Bole sub city and for future researcher. The analysis of employees and customers implies that there are different challenges to ensure good governance, the sub city land development and management office shall improve the practice of good governance on the service outlet in order to improve the office's service quality and to achieve organizational goals. As result based on summary and conclusion for this research the researcher put forward the following recommendation.

5.3.1. For Sub City Leaders

- The office introduced BPR, BSC and citizen charter for employees and customers to facilitate them to exercise their right and responsibilities as well. To give clear information
- To develop clarity when newly enacted laws, rules and directive for employees and service users
- To make the service standards up to date and compatible with real situations, it is recommended to evaluate their output and
- Additionally the office constantly to give training, monitoring, evaluating the output, based on evaluation result, rewarding good performing employees and taking corrective measure those who utilize the official place for their own gains.
- For the improvement of good governance practice, employees and customer participation is important. So, the sub city land development and management office have to engage the resident and

stockholders on formulating plans, policies, charters implementation, evaluations period and during decision making.

- Leaders should have to be committed enough to participate the stockholders.
- Employees must participate different short term and long term training courses because behavior of employees is frequently helpful in bring about preferred result.
- In relation with efficiency the rules directives and procedures, the office has to make on job monitoring and evaluation to fill their gaps and to make periodic improvements. Availability of accurate, integrated and computerized land registration is important for efficient and availability of one stop shop for facilitate service and responsible bodies are competent in managing to convince all settlers to comply with redevelopment programs as effective service. The foundation of a successful land administration system is reliable land records. So, the office should be formulating this system. To improve the inconsistency problem between the office's professionals on interpreting land related law, the sub city office should put a work direction and procedure.
- The office required necessary materials which assist in administrating the land effectively
- The finding of the study shows that leaders of the sub city were less effective, poorly committed to meet organizational goal. Therefore it needs to have effective leader in order to promote good governance and sustainable development.

For Future Researcher

- This research had intended to establish the Practice and Challenges of Good Governance in Bole Sub City Land Development and Management office. Other researcher who has interest to employ research in land Development and Management office may focus on effect of good governance on customer satisfaction in the sub city.

Reference

Abdellatif, A. (2003) *Good Governance and its relationship to Democrat and Economic Development*: Republic of Korea.

Abdi Mohmmad. (2010) *Literature Review and Research Problem* Addis Ababa, Ethiopia, Civil Service University, Un published.

ADB (1999), African Development Bank, (ADF) African Development Fund: Bank Group Policy on Good Governance Accessed in :http:/ www,afdb,org/fileadmin/uploads/afdb/Documents/policy-Documents/21-EN-Bank Group Policy on Good Governance pdf, retrieved on 11/12/2014.

ADB (1999). African Development Bank, African Development Fund.

Africa Development Bank and Africa Development Fund, (2009) *Country Governance Profile*, Addis Ababa.

Akram, K..(1988)*Ethiopian Public Administration, Governance and Ethics*

ARD, Inc. (2004), Ethiopia Land Policy and Administration Assessment, Final Report with Appendices, USAID Contract No LAG-00-98-00031-00, Task Order No.4 Addis Ababa Ethiopia.

Azeb, W. (2006) *Assessment of the Status of good Governance in Public sector* in Debre Elias Woreda Amhara National Regional State. Bangkok, Thailand.

Bank Group Policy on good governance accessed in http:/www.afdb/fileadmin/uplads/afdb/Documents/Policy-Documents/21-EN-Bank Group Policy on Good Governance pdf. Retrived on 11/1214.

Bell, C.K, (2007), Good Governance in Land Administration, Strategic Integration of Surveying Services- First Working Week for the new FIG Council a big success, Hong Kong, China (SAR, International Federation of Surveyors (FIG).

Bole Sub City, (2016/17) *Annual Report.*

Brhanu Demisse (2014), Challenges of applying good governance in land administration: in the case of Gindo Town, MA Thesis Ethiopian Civil Service University, Addis Ababa.

BRUCE, J.W. (1998) Reviced of Land tenure terminology, Tenure Brief, No 1, land Tenure Center, University of Wisconsin, Madison.

Bryman, A. and Bell, E. (2003) Business Research Method. Oxford University Press.

Central Statistics Agency (CSA), (2007*) Population and Housing Census* 2007 Report, Addis Ababa Region.

Crouch, L. and Donald, W. (2008). *Governance, Management and Financing of Education for All:* Basic Frame works and Case Studies.

David Palmer, Szilard Fricska, Babette Wehrmann (2009), Towards Improved Land Governance, Land Tenure Working paper 11, Compensation Payment, Available in; http/www/.cepes,ro/publications/degualt,htm,accessed on 14/10/2014.

Dhaliwal, S. (2004) *Good governance in Local self government*, New Delhi: Rajour Garden.

Doebele, W.A. ((1982), Land Readjustment: A different approach to financing Urbanization.

Duran, M.A. Morales (2004), The Economics of Favoritism working paper university of Malage.

Economic Commission for Africa (ECA), (2005), *African Governance report*: Addis Ababa, Ethiopia.

Engda Esayas (2010), Urban Land use Planning and management in Ethiopia, VDM verlag Dr. Muller GmbH and CO.KG, USA.

FAO (2007), Food and Agriculture Organization of the United Nation, Good Governance in Land Tenure and Administration, FAO Land Tenure Studies, 9, Rome.

FAO (2007), Gender and Land Tenure Rome, Food and Agriculture Organization of the United Nations (FAO).

FDRE (2011), The Government of the Federal Democratic Republic of Ethiopia: A Proclamation to Provide for lease holding of urban lands; proclamation No 721/2011, Federal Negarit Gazeta, Addis Ababa.

FDRE (Constitution (1995), Federal Democratic Republic of Ethiopia Constitution, Addis Ababa, Ethiopia.

FIG (2010), Land Governance in support of the Millennium Development Goals, FIG/World Bank Conference Washington DC, USA.

Fraenke and Wallen, (2008:148) *How to design and evaluate research in education* (7th ed.). McGraw-Hill Humanities/Social sciences/.

Girma Bonsa (2013), An Assessment of Urban Land Administration from Good Governance Perspective: Case Study of Sebeta City Administration, MA thesis, Ethiopian Civil Service University.

Governance in Africa (2015) *challenges and prospects, International Meeting Process for Debate and Proposals on Governance*, www.institute governance.org/en/chapitrage/fiche-64.html(accessed on April, 5, 2015).

Grindle, M. (2004) *"Good Governance: Poverty Reduction and Reform in Developing Countries"* Governance: An International Journal of Policy Administration and Institution 17 (4); 525-48 doi: 10.111/1.0952-1895-2004.0025.x.

Grindle, M. (2007) *Good Enough Governance Revisited" Development policy* Review 25(5)-74 doi:10.1111/j.1467-7679.2007.00385.xed. Boston person

Haradhan, M. (2017)*Two Criteria for Good Measurements in Research*: Validity and Reliability: Premier University, Chittagong, Bangladesh. Online At Https://Mpra.Ub.Uni-Muenchen.De/83458/ MPRA Paper No. 83458, Posted 24 December 2017 08:48 Utcannals of Spiru Haret University, 17(3): 58-82.

Hilal, A. (2014)*Constraints and impediments of good governance:* future prospects, Malaysia.

Kassahun, Y. (2010) *Assessment of the Prevalence of good governance in public sectors*, the case of Debre Berhan Town, Ethiopia.

Kothari, C.R. (1990). Research Methodology: Methods and Techniques (2nd revised Ed.). New Delhi: New Age International Publishers.

Kothari, C.R. (2004) *Research Methodology: Methods and techniques*, Second Revised Edition: New Age international Publisher, New Delhi.

Kothari., C. (2008).*Research Methodology, Methods and Techniques*, 2nd ed.(109-110).

Kumar, R. (2011) Research *Methodology*: A Step By Step Guide For Beginners: 3rd Ed. New Delhi, India: Sage Publications India Pvt. Ltd.

Liyang Qian (2014), Evaluating Land Administration System from the Perspective of Good Governance; a case study of informal settlement in Kathmandu Balley, MXC Thesis in Geo Information Science and Earth Observation, University of Twente, Enschede, Netherlands.

Lulit Hailemeskel (2011), Assessment of Land Administration Service Delivery in two Selected Services: Title deed/ownership Certificate and Compensation Services: In Arada Sub city of Addis Ababa, MA Thesis, Addis Ababa University, Ethiopia.

Map of Addis Ababa city Administration, with its 10 sub-cities.

Melese, D. (2013) *The practice and challenges of good governance in public institutions*, South Nations Nationality of People, Ethiopia.

Mercy Crops, (2010) *Guide to good governance programming Methodological issues in the evaluation of progress* at the National and Local levels.

Muhammad, A. (2015) *Governance and Good Governance*: A conceptual perspective University of Karachi.

Mulusew, A. (2013) *Assessment of good governance* in Ethiopia Civil Service in the case of Ethiopia Ministry of Civil Service.

Plummer, Janelle (2012), Diagnosing Corruption in Ethiopia: Perceptions, Realities, and the way forward, Washington, DC: World Bank, DOI 10, 1596/978-0-8213-9531-8.

Quian, Y. (2003) *How Reform worked in China*; in Rodrik

Ram, P. (2017) *Challenges and Prospects of Good Governance in reduction of Poverty*: A case study of Buee Town 10 Kebele, Ethiopia, Global Journal of Political Science and Administration Vol. 5, No. 3, pp. 13-27, June 2017

Samsudin, S. (2011) "A Reviewed or organization arrangements in Malaysia Land Administration system to wards good governance issues and challenges" brigging the gap between cultures, FIG working week, 18-22 may 2011 Marraketh, Morocco.

Shrestha, B. (2000). *Good Governance in Nepal, Perspective form- Panchthar an*

Singh, K. (2007) *Quantitative Social research methods.*

Smith, B. (2007) *Good Governance and development.*

Suchitra, P.(2004) *Commitment to good governance, development and poverty reduction :* methodological issues in the evaluation of progress at the national and local levels. Bangkok, Thailand.

Suresh Joshi (2014), Assessment of Land Governance: A case of Urban Land Readjustment, MSC Thesis in Geo Information Science and Earth Observation.

UNDP, (2009) *Governance for Sustainable Development*

UNECE (2005), Land Administration in the UNECE Region: Development Trends and Main Principles, New York and Geneva.

UNFPA (2007), State of World Population 2007- Unleashing the potential of Urban Growth.

UNFPA (2007), State of World Population 2007- Unleashing the potential of Urban Growth.

UN-HABITAT (2007), Transparency in Land Administration a capacity building agenda for Africa, Expert Group Meeting on Transparency in Land Administration, Nairobi, Kenya (UN-HABITAT).

UN-HABITAT (2007), Transparency in Land Administration, a capacity building agenda for Africa, Expert Group Meeting on Transparency in Land Administration, Nairobi, Kenya (UN-HABITAT).

United Nation Development Program UNDP, (2009) *Governance for sustainable Development.*

United Nation Development program, (1997) *Governance for Sustainable Human Development* UNDP policy Document.

United Nation Development Program, (2012) *Governance for Sustainable Development Integrating Governance in the Post-*2015 Development Framework, New York.

United Nation Development Program, UNDP (1997) Governance and sustainable human development.

United Nation, (2007) *Good Governance practices for the protection of Human rights.* New

United Nations Development Program Oslo Governance Centre, (2009) *Planning A Governance Assessment:* A Guide to approaches, Costs and benefit, Norway

United Nations Economic and Social Commission for Asia and the pacific (UNESCAP) (Un dated). Accessed from http:www.unescap,prg/sites/default/files/good governance :pdf, retrieved on 25/12/2014

United State Agency for International Development (USAID), (2005) *Land Tenure, property Rights, and Local Land Governance*; http://www.usaid.gov/who-we-are/agency-policy/serious-5oo

Williamson I. Enemark S. Wallance J. and Rajabifard A. (2010), Land Administration for Sustainable Development ESRI press Academic, Redlands, California.

Williamson, I.P, (2001), Land Administration: Best Practice" providing the infrastructure for land policy implementation, Land Use Policy, 18 (4). woredas.http:/*/www.ilic.gov.et/index.php/en/administrative-boundaries.*

World Bank (1992) *Governance and Development*, Washington DC, World Bank.

World Bank, WB (1999). Entering the 21th Century: World Development Report 1999/2000, Washington D.E: Oxford University Press.

Zakout, W, Wehrmann B, & Torhonen M-P, (2006), Good Governance in Land Administration: Principles and Good Practices, Washington Dc\.C. (World Bank and FAO).

Zelalem, T. (2016 *Practice and challenges of Good Governance in Land Administration* in the case of Yeka Sub city. Addis Ababa Ethiopia.

List of Acronyms

ADB	:	African Development Bank
ADF	:	African Development Fund
AU	:	Africa Union
CSA	:	Central Statistics Authority
CSRP-	:	Civil-Service Reform Program
ECA-	:	Economic Commission for Africa
FAO	:	Food and Agriculture Organization
FDRE	:	Federal Democratic Republic Of Ethiopia for Asia and the Pacific
GTP-	:	Growth and Transformation Plan
ICT	:	Information Communication Technology
MoFED	:	Ministry of Finance and Economic Development
SPSS-	:	Statistical package for the Social Sciences
UN	:	United Nation
UNDP	:	United Nation Development Programs:
UNECE	:	United Nation Economic of Ethiopia
UNESCAP	:	United Nations, Economic and Social Commission
UNHABITAT	:	United Nations Human Settlement Program
USAID	:	United State Agency for International Development

Index